2030 Second Coming

Daniel Speck

"This Jesus, who has been taken up from you into heaven, will come in just the same way as you have watched Him go into heaven." Acts 1:11

Cover Photo: The Mount of Olives as seen from the Temple Mount in Jerusalem. This is the place where Jesus Christ ascended to heaven in 30 AD and will return to in 2030. Photo by the author.

Chapters

Introduction

One thousand nine hundred eighty four years ago Jesus Christ was crucified, rose from the dead and ascended into heaven. He promised to return one day. He also said no man would know the day or hour, but He never said that that no man would know the year.

The first step in understanding Biblical Prophecy

You must be born again. A sincere faith in Jesus Christ resulting in a new birth is absolutely necessary to understanding Last Days prophecy. **"'You must be born again.'…For God so loved the world that He gave His only begotten Son, that whoever believes in Him will not perish, but have eternal life."** John 3:7,16.

Salvation is by grace through faith alone

For by grace you have been saved through faith; and that not of yourselves, it is the gift of God, not as a result of works, so that no one should boast. Ephesians 2:7.

You can be assured of always being saved

When you receive Christ through faith you can be absolutely sure that you will be with the Lord forever. **"I give them eternal life and they will never perish and no one will snatch them out of my hand."** John 10:28.

You can be saved today

If you haven't yet received Jesus Christ as your Savior or not are sure that you are saved, there is no better time than now to make sure. Here is a prayer you can say to receive Jesus through faith to be saved and born again:

"Lord Jesus, I am a sinner and I need a Savior. I believe You died for my sins and rose from the dead. Come into my heart and give me the free gift of eternal life. Thank You."

If you have said a prayer like this and sincerely believed, you can be sure that all your sins are forgiven, you are going to heaven, and you are born again.

You are baptized in the Holy Spirit the moment you believe

You too, after hearing the Word of Truth, the good news of your salvation, have been sealed with the promised Holy Spirit. Ephesians 1:13.

The Holy Spirit unlocks the mysteries of Biblical prophecy

But we speak God's wisdom in a mystery. The hidden wisdom which God predestined before the ages for our glory; that wisdom which none of the rulers of this world has understood... for to us God revealed them through the Spirt...but a natural man does not accept the things of the Spirit of God, for they are foolishness to him; and he cannot understand them because they are spiritually appraised. I Corinthians 2:7,10,14.

Jesus is Faithful and True

"Behold a white horse, and He who sits upon it is faithful and true." Revelation 19:11

"Heaven and earth will pass away, but My words will never pass away." Jesus Christ, Matthew 24:35.

In Jesus Christ we have a Savior who is absolutely trustworthy. Anything or anyone else we put our trust in is going to fail us but He never will. He is the way to know God, He is the truth we can rest our lives upon, and He is the assurance of life everlasting. He promised to return and no matter if the whole world says otherwise, He will return.

The Written Word Alone

The sole authority and source for revelation, doctrine and prophecy is the written Word of God. All extra-Biblical sources for prophecy or revelation are false. The final chapter of the Bible ends all prophecy: **"I testify to everyone who hears the words of the prophecy of this book: if anyone adds to them, God will add to him the plagues which are written in this book."** Revelation 22:18.

Chapter One

The Glorious Return of Jesus Christ

Yes, it is really going to happen. Not invisibly, not symbolically and not instantaneously. And if you are saved today, you will probably be here when it does. It won't be the end of the world but it will certainly be the end of history as we know it. It will forever, radically change every person on the planet and what they understand as reality. Every false religion, philosophy and ideology will be obliterated in a single day. Darwinism will cease to exist. Atheism will instantly disappear. Not one individual on earth will ever again have any doubt about who God really is.

It will be big. It will be awesome beyond description. It will be loud. It will be beautiful. It will be more than most people can bear. The strongest and bravest men will hide themselves in terror. Billions of people all over the planet will be screaming, weeping and trying to find a hole to crawl into.

But if you are a born-again believer, your experience will be completely different. It will be the best day of your life. You will see Jesus your Savior in all His glory coming on the clouds with His mighty angels in flaming fire. He has come back for you just as He promised. Your body will be instantly transformed into a glorious, strong and indestructible one. You will see other believers come out of their graves in their new bodies. You will see them rise into the sky to meet the Lord. Then you will feel yourself rise into the air as well. The whole world will be watching. Everyone will see it. You will not be able to contain yourself. You will shout with joy like you have never shouted before.

Scriptural wealth of the Second Coming and Rapture

There is a rich bounty of Scripture which details all the events of our Lord's return and our gathering with Him in the air:

"And they will see the Son of Man coming on the clouds of the sky with power and great glory. And He will send forth His angels with a great trumpet and they will gather together His elect from the four winds, from one end of the sky to the other." Matthew 24:30-31.

"For the Lord Himself will descend from heaven with a shout, with the voice of the archangel and with the trumpet of God, and the dead in Christ will rise first. Then we who are alive and remain will be caught up together with them in the clouds to meet the Lord in the air, and so we shall always be with the Lord." I Thessalonians 4:16-18.

"Behold He is coming with the clouds and every eye will see Him, even those who pierced Him; and all the tribes of the earth will mourn over Him." Revelation 1:7.

"I was watching in the night visions, and behold, One like the Son of Man coming with the clouds of heaven! ...and the time arrived when the saints took possession of the kingdom." Daniel 7:13,22 (NKJV).

Even with all the wealth of clear Biblical statements like these, there is still more about the Second Coming and Rapture for us to discover in the prophetic pictures hidden the stories of the Hebrew and New Testament Scriptures. In these stories are unmistakable clues to not only to a better understanding of this event but even to the exact year it was prophesied to happen.

Chapter Two

Why Jesus Will Return in 2030

In the year 2030 Jesus will return on the clouds to resurrect the dead in Christ and rapture the Church and every eye shall see Him.

The prophetic pictures of the life of Jesus

The stories of the life of Jesus often had deeper prophetic meaning. The Lord painted pictures of future events with many of the things He did in the Gospels. Since the first century, clues to the mystery of the year of His return lie hidden in these stories and with the help of the gifts of the Holy Spirit, they can be understood.

The woman at the well

Jesus and His disciples stop at Jacob's well in Samaria. While the twelve go into the nearby town to buy food, a Samaritan woman comes to draw water. He asks her for a drink and says, **"If you knew the gift of God and who it is who says to you, 'Give Me a drink," you would have asked Him and He would have given you living water."** He then proceeds to discuss His living water with her. She acts incredulous until He tells her,

"Go call your husband here." She says, "I have no husband." He tells her, "You have correctly said, 'I have no husband'; for you have had five husbands and the one whom you have now is not your husband; this you said truly." She says, "I know the Messiah is coming..." He answers, "I who speak to you am He." The Samaritan woman then drops her jar and goes into the town and tells her neighbors, "Come see a man who told me all the things I have done; this is not the Christ, is it?" After listening to the Lord themselves, many in the town also believe and invite Him to stay; "...and He stayed there two days." John 4: 7-43.

This wonderful story has been a favorite of so many Christians down through the ages. It shows how Jesus personally engaged people from all walks of life and every ethnic group; even the outcasts of society. He took the time to sit down and minister to women as well as men; very unusual for a rabbi of His day. His disciples appear shocked and somewhat put out because He was not only talking to a woman alone, but a gentile woman, and incredibly, a Samaritan woman, and even more, a woman caught up in serious sin.

But to me the most amazing thing about this story is that He revealed things to this woman, this sinful, adulterous Gentile that had just met Him, that He hadn't even revealed to His disciples yet! He was explaining to her the deepest mysteries of God, including the baptism of the Holy Spirit, which none of the Twelve would fully understand until years later on the day of Pentecost.

The words of Jesus took root in this woman's heart and she turned from her sins to faith in Him. In fact it was this Samaritan woman who evangelized the town and led her neighbors to Christ. The disciples had just come from there but did nothing but buy food. They were fruitless, while she bore fruit. Her eyes were opened while they remained blind. They were angry and jealous, while she helped bring others into the Kingdom of God.

He stayed two days with the woman at the well

The Lord's two day stay with the woman at the well may have little meaning for the casual reader but it is immensely important when the prophetic picture of this story is fully understood. The Samaritan woman is a prophetic type of the Church, whom Jesus offers the gift of living water that, **"...will become in him a well of water springing up to eternal life."** John 4:13. He is talking about the baptism of the Holy Spirit here; His gift to the Church and His gift to every born-again believer.

"After two days He went out from there..."

These two days are an important detail in the prophetic

picture that the Lord is painting here. Often the smallest details in the Scriptures can take us much deeper into understanding God's mysteries.

Peter's time scale for the Second Coming

The Apostle Peter's second letter provides us with a key which unlocks the deeper meaning of the two days that Jesus spent with the Samaritans of Sychar.

"Know this first of all, that in the last days mockers will come with their mocking, following after their own lusts and saying, 'Where is the promise of His coming?'...But do not let this one fact escape your notice, beloved, that <u>with the Lord one day is like a thousand years and a thousand years like one day</u>." II Peter 3:3,8.

Peter answered the question of when the promise of Christ's coming will be fulfilled with a simple mathematical formula: one day = one thousand years. He repeats it forwards and backwards, suggesting that this is not just an approximation, but an exact number. With this key in hand we can unlock the prophetic picture the Lord painted with His two day stay in Samaria: the Church age will last for two thousand years after which He will "go forth."

Using this prophetic type, we can identify the exact year of Christ's return. The Church age began in the year 30 AD after the ascension of the Lord and the outpouring of the Holy Spirit on the day of Pentecost. 2030 is two thousand years after that, so we certainly can expect Christ to return in the year 2030.

No man will know the day or hour

Even though we can know the year, we don't want to make the mistake of believing that any man can know the day of His return.

"But of that day and hour no one knows, not even the angels in heaven, nor the Son, but the Father alone." Matthew 24:36.

Even knowing the year, the return of the Lord will still be a sudden event without immediate warning. A wonderful but anticipated surprise for believers and a terrifying shock for those who have received the mark of the beast.

Chapter Three

Raising Lazarus After Two Days

On the surface, the Gospel of John has little to say about the return of Christ or the Last Days, but when the types and symbols in John are carefully studied, it proves to be one of the richest books in the New Testament for Second Coming prophetic revelation.

The story of Jesus raising Lazarus from the dead in John 11 is one of the most amazingly detailed prophetic pictures of the return of the Lord. It begins when the Jews of Jerusalem threaten to stone Him so He leaves the city and goes over to the east bank of the Jordan River. There word comes that His friend Lazarus is sick. The narrative then says, **"So when He heard that he was sick, He stayed <u>two days</u> longer in the place where He was."**

After the two days, the Lord traveled up to Bethany where Lazarus's sister, Martha came out to meet Him. Understanding His power to heal the sick she said, **"Lord if you had been here, my brother would not have died."** But He has even greater power than this and tells her, **"I am the resurrection and the life, he who believes in Me will live even if he dies, and everyone who lives and believes in Me will never die."**

Martha then went back to the house and called her sister Mary, **"...saying secretly, 'The Teacher is here and is calling you.' And when she heard it, she got up quickly and was coming to Him."**

Martha and Mary then follow Jesus to the tomb where the body of Lazarus lay. The Lord cried out with a loud voice, **"Lazarus, come forth!"** and the dead man walked out the grave.

A complete picture of the Second Coming

We can read I Thessalonians 4 along with this story and see the exact parallels with the Rapture and Second Coming events.

"For the Lord Himself will descend from heaven with a shout, with the voice of the archangel, and the trumpet of God, and the dead in Christ will rise first, then we who are alive and remain will be caught up together in the clouds to meet the Lord in the air, and so we shall always be with the Lord." I Thessalonians 4:16-18.

Martha came out to meet Jesus first. He tells her that He Himself is the resurrection. Martha is a type of the dead in Christ who rise first in the First Resurrection.

Then Mary came out to meet Him. When she heard that He was coming, "...**she got up quickly and was coming to Him**." The Greek word "harpazo" (translated as rapture) means to snatch away quickly. John makes the point that Mary got up quickly, a graphic picture of the Church being snatched away with

Christ at His return. Mary is a type of the rapture of the Church.

Martha and Mary: the First Resurrection and the Rapture of the Church

First the dead in Christ are raised at His return just like the resurrection the Lord promised Mary, then the living believers will be caught up to meet them in the air, just like the way Mary got up quickly and went out to meet Him. But there is one more thing that the Lord will accomplish when He returns: the restoration of the nation of Israel.

"He brought me out by the Spirit of the Lord and set me down in the middle of the valley; and it was full of bones...Then He said to me, 'Son of man, these bones are the whole house of Israel...Behold I will open your graves and cause you to come out of your graves, My people, and I will bring you into the land of Israel.'" Ezekiel 37:1-12.

"He will revive us after two days, He will raise us up on the third day, that we may live before Him." Hosea 6:2.

Lazarus: a prophetic type of the nation of Israel

And finally, Lazarus is raised from the dead. For two thousand years the Jews as a nation have been spiritually dead but when they see the Lord Jesus return on the clouds then all Israel will believe in Him as Messiah, Savior and Lord:

"**Behold He is coming on the clouds and every eye will see Him, even those** *(Israel)* **who pierced Him.**" Revelation 1:7.

"**I will pour out on the house of David and on the inhabitants of Jerusalem, the Spirit of grace and of supplication, so that they will look on Me whom they have pierced.**" Zechariah 12:10.

"**The sons of Israel will return and seek the Lord their God and David their King; and they will come trembling to the Lord and to His goodness in the Last Days.**" Hosea 3:5

So there are three things the Lord will accomplish when He returns:

1. Raise the dead in Christ

2. Gather up the Church in the Rapture

3. Revive and restore Israel, the Jewish nation

Crossing the Jordan

There is one more important detail in this story that can be easily overlooked. Jesus is on the east side of the Jordan River when word is sent that Lazarus is sick. He must cross it to go over to Bethany. The Jordan has very important symbolism throughout the Bible. We see from the Hebrew Scriptures that whenever a Messianic type crossed the Jordan River, a picture of the Second Coming was being painted. Joshua as a type of Christ, crossed the Jordan to bring Israel into the Promised Land. David as a type of the Messiah crossed the

Jordan to restore his kingdom after the defeat of Absalom. And Jehu, a type of the Lion of Judah, crossed the Jordan River to execute judgment on the enemies of God.

The Jordan itself is a prophetic type of the Tribulation. It was a flooded barrier that Israel crossed by the miraculous hand of God, just as they did at the Red Sea.

Two days or two thousand years until He returns

But before crossing the Jordan River, Jesus deliberately stayed on the east bank two more days after hearing the news that Lazarus was sick. This two day delay has always been an enigma. It is a particular and exact number and numbers have very important symbolic meaning in the Bible. But with the picture of Christ's return graphically laid out for us in this story, together with Peter's time key, this has to be another prophecy that the Lord will return to raise the dead, rapture the Church and restore Israel after two thousand years.

Chapter Four

The Good Samaritan's Promise

There is at least one more story in the Gospels that speaks of the return of the Lord after two days: the parable of the Good Samaritan.

Most people know what it means to be a good Samaritan because this story is very popular in Christian cultures. On its surface, it is about being a good neighbor and caring for others. The deeper meaning of this story, however, is a little understood mystery.

A man is beaten by robbers on his way from Jerusalem to Jericho and left half dead. A priest, then a Levite pass by on the other side. **"But a Samaritan, who was on a journey, came upon him; and when he saw him, he felt compassion, and came to him and bandaged up his wounds, pouring oil and wine on them; and he put him on his own beast, and brought him to an inn and took care of him.**

On the next day he took out two denarii and gave them to the innkeeper and said, 'Take care of him; and whatever more you spend, when I return I will repay you.'" Luke 10:33-35.

The good Samaritan is a prophetic picture of Jesus Himself. He is the one who has compassion on the wounded man and gives the innkeeper two denarii to care for him. An important point of the story is that the Samaritan promised to return and settle the account. This is a metaphor for the Second Coming. The two denarii is a key detail as well. One denarius was equal to a day's wage at the time. A one day stay at the average hotel today costs on average, about day's wage. The same must have been true in first century Israel, so two denarii would be enough for two day's stay at an inn, meaning that the good Samaritan intended to return after two days.

Using Peter's Second Coming time scale, we can unlock this mystery: hidden in this story is another prophecy of the two thousand years until the Lord Jesus will return.

Filling in the rest of the prophetic types here, the wounded man represents Israel in its wounded spiritual condition which the religious authorities of the time were unable and unwilling to help. The journey from Jerusalem to Jericho is the sinful direction Israel was traveling, from the Kingdom of God to the kingdom of the world. It is Jesus who cares for the man and takes him to the innkeeper, a type of the Church. Spiritually, Israel is wounded and half dead, and it is the Church who cares for Israel and has taken on their burden of bearing fruit for the Kingdom (Matthew 21:43).

Just as in the story of the Good Samaritan, Christ will return after two thousand years to reward the Church and restore Israel.

Chapter Five

Hosea Predicted the Exact Year!

Hosea prophesied of the return of Jesus:

"I will go away and return to My place until they acknowledge their guilt and seek my face; in their affliction they will earnestly seek Me." "Come, let us return to the Lord, for He has torn us, but He will heal us; He has wounded us, but He will bandage us. He will revive us after two days; He will raise us up on the third day..." Hosea 5:15-6:2.

The Lord Jesus returned to His place when He ascended into heaven from the Mount of Olives. He will not come back until the Jews as a nation believe in Him as their Savior and Messiah. Using our II Peter time key for the Second Coming, we can unlock the mystery of Hosea 6:2. It reveals that Israel will be revived two thousand years after He left and raised up in the third millennium after.

Only one particular year can fulfill Hosea's prophecy

The revival is when Israel comes to faith in Christ, and being raised up is the restoration of Israel as a nation. Since Jesus Christ is going to accomplish both of these events in the same year when He returns, there is only one possible year when this prophecy can be fulfilled. That must to be the single year in which the second millennium after Christ's ascension ends and the third millennium begins, which is the year 2030.

2030 marks two thousand years after Jesus **"returned to His place"** in 30 AD, but is also the beginning of the third millennium "day" after He ascended. There is no other possible year when Hosea's prophecy of the Second Coming can be fulfilled.

Two part return in 2030

This story also confirms the two part coming of Christ. When Jesus appears on the clouds to gather the Church into heaven then **"...every eye will see Him, even those who pierced Him."** (Israel). This is the time of the spiritual revival of Israel, when every Jewish person in the world will believe in Jesus after they see Him coming in His glory. Then the Lord will come back again to raise up Israel. This is the White Horse return when He comes permanently to fully restore Israel as a nation. Both of these events must happen sometime between the day of Pentecost and the Feast of Booths in 2030. The Cloud Appearance will occur sometime at the end of the second millennium after the Church age began, and the White Horse Return will happen after the third millennium begins.

2,000 cubits behind

There is at least one more example where the two thousand year time before Christ's return can be seen in Scripture. When Israel is about to cross the Jordan River into the Promised Land, Joshua instructs them: **"When you see the ark of the covenant of the Lord your God with the Levitical priests carrying it, then you shall set out from your place and go after it. However, <u>there shall be between you and it a distance of about 2,000 cubits</u> by measure.**

Do not come near it, that you may know the way by which you shall go, for you have not passed this way before." Joshua 3: 3-4. This may be a prophetic picture of the 2,000 years that would pass before Israel comes to faith in the Lord Jesus.

No one can know the day or hour

Even though the year of Christ's return can be known through the prophetic pictures the Lord has given us in the Gospels and the Prophets, His coming will still be like a thief in the night and no man will know the day or hour. It will be a complete surprise for unbelievers, but believers will certainly know when He is near.

"**But of that day and hour no one knows...**" Matthew 24:36.

"**For you yourselves know full well that the Day of the Lord will come just like a thief in the night. While they are saying, "Peace and safety!" then destruction will come upon them suddenly like labor pains upon a woman with child, and they will not escape. But you, brethren, are not in darkness that the day would overtake you like a thief...**" II Thessalonians 5:1-4.

We, the Church are going to know when it is near because of the events prophesied to happen just before He returns.

"**But when you see these things** *(of the Tribulation)* **begin to take place, straighten up and lift up your heads, because your redemption is drawing near.**" Luke 21:28.

Chapter Six

The Battle of Jericho and 2023

The Tribulation will begin 7 Years before the Lord Returns in 2030.

"But immediately <u>after</u> the tribulation of those days...they will see the Son of Man coming on the clouds of the sky with great power and glory." Matthew 24:29,30.

The Lord makes it clear that He will return immediately after the Tribulation at the Last Trumpet, the Seventh Trumpet of Revelation. Matthew 24:20-31, I Corinthians 15:51, Revelation 10:7, Colossians 1:26-27.

The Tribulation will last for seven years (Daniel 9:27) and by subtracting 7 years from the end of the 2000 year Church age in 2030, will place the beginning of the Tribulation in 2023.

2023 is 70 Jubilees after the Battle of Jericho

The year **2023** will also mark 70 Jubilees since Israel entered the promised land and conquered Jericho. In biblical numerology, 70 marks a full completion of time. Jubilees occur every 49 years when the fields were rested, each family returned to their land, debts were cancelled and slaves were set free (Leviticus 25:8-11).

The Battle of Jericho is a prophetic type of the battle for the Kingdom of the World during the Tribulation. Rahab, a prophetic type of the Gentile Bride, the Church, was taken out with a shout on the Seventh Day after the Seventh Trumpet just as the Church will be Raptured with a shout after the Seven Seals at the Seventh Trumpet.

Seventy is the number of a full completion of time in biblical numerology:

70 years for a normal life span
70 centuries for world history to be completed
70 years until the Babylonian captivity was over
70 "weeks" decreed for Israel's completed redemption (Daniel 9:24-27)
70 Jubilees (7X7X70) from Israel's entrance in to the Promised Land until Daniel's 70th week begins (2023)

In 2023 there will have been a total of 70 jubilees since Israel crossed the Jordan into the Promised Land in 1406 BC:* 7x7x70=3430-1406=2024-1=2023+7=2030 (there is no year 0, so we subtract 1 year* from 2024). In other words, 70 Jubilees plus 7 will mark the year of Christ's Second Coming (7x7x70+7) in 2030.

The 70 weeks of Daniel 9

Daniel's famous 70 weeks also points to the exact year that the Tribulation will begin.

24 "<u>Seventy weeks have been decreed for your people</u> and your holy city, to finish the

transgression, to make an end of sin, to make atonement for iniquity, to bring in everlasting righteousness, to seal up vision and prophecy and to anoint the most holy place. 25 "So you are to know and discern that from the issuing of a decree to restore and rebuild Jerusalem <u>until Messiah the Prince there will be seven weeks and sixty-two weeks</u>; it will be built again, with plaza and moat, even in times of distress. 26 "<u>Then after the sixty-two weeks the Messiah will be cut off</u> and have nothing, and the people of the prince who is to come will destroy the city and the sanctuary. And its end will come with a flood; even to the end there will be war; desolations are determined. 27 "And he will make <u>a firm covenant with the many for one week, but in the middle of the week</u> he will put a stop to sacrifice and grain offering; and on the wing of <u>abominations will come one who makes desolate</u>, even until a complete destruction, one that is decreed, is poured out on the one who makes desolate." Daniel 9:24-27.

Adding up the years until the end

7 + 62 "weeks" (483 years) until the Messiah is cut off in 30 AD + 2000 years (the Kingdom temporarily is taken from Israel and given to the Church) + 1 "week," or 7 years, is 2030 when Jesus returns. In the middle of the 70th "week" the Abomination of Desolation will occur (Matthew 24:15).

Calculation notes

*Israel left Egypt in 1446 BC, and ate manna in the wilderness for 40 years (Exodus 16:35) until they crossed the Jordan into Canaan. This puts their entrance into the Promised Land and the beginning of the 49 year Jubilee cycles in the year 1406 BC. I Kings 6:1 states that Solomon began to build the Temple 480 years after Israel left Egypt. The Temple was started in 966 BC so 966+480=1446-40=1406 BC. Jubilees are announced with a trumpet on the Day of Atonement, which occurs during the fall on the tenth day of the seventh month (Hebrew calendar).

*Calculating dates that span BC and AD:

3, 2, 1 BC, 1, 2, 3 AD =5 total years because there is no year zero so one year must be subtracted from the sum total of the two dates (3BC + 3AD =6 -1=5 total years).

Chapter Seven

Pharaoh's dream and 2016

After Joseph was sold into Egypt by his brothers, the Pharaoh had a dream of seven fat cows who were eaten by seven thin cows. Joseph was summoned from prison for his ability to interpret dreams. His interpretation of Pharaoh's dream told of a seven year famine that was about to come upon the whole world. It also told of a seven year period of abundance and prosperity that would immediately precede the famine. Joseph was then given the responsibility to gather grain during this seven year agricultural boom as a savings account against the prophesied seven years of severe famine.

In the end, Joseph was used to not only enrich the house of Pharaoh, but to save his own family as well. The story ends with Joseph reconciled with his brothers and father in Egypt where they prosper and grow to become the nation of Israel.

Famine in the Hebrew Scriptures is symbolic of the Tribulation

Famine, especially a seven year famine is a prophetic type of the seven year Tribulation period that will immediately precede the coming of Christ. But Pharaoh's dream has another aspect that is not precisely detailed in any other biblical description of the Tribulation: seven years of abundant harvest.

The seven years of good harvest in Pharaoh's dream allowed Joseph to save and prepare for the seven years of famine. If there is to be seven years of abundance just before the Tribulation, it is obviously to be a time of preparation, a period of grace to prepare the saints for the difficult time to come.

Seven years prior to the beginning of the Tribulation in 2023 is the year 2016. This is the year that believers should begin to prepare for the Seven Seals, spiritually and strategically as well. Stocking food, getting out of debt, learning how to grow your own crops and make your own energy, etc. Being part of a network of underground believers will be important as well. Plan on continuing to preach the Gospel, not just going into a bunker and waiting it out. Get your relationship with Christ in good order and memorize those Scripture you will need against the day when owning a Bible is outlawed. The Church will also be responsible to help protect the Jews and be a witness to Christ among them.

Biblical principles of obedient preparation

1. Joseph was given 7 years of plenty to prepare for the 7 year famine. He stored up 20% of all of Egypt's abundant harvest for 7 years against the 7 years of prophesied famine.
2. Noah was warned to prepare food and enter the ark 7 days before the flood began
3. Rahab was warned 7 days before the 7 day battle of Jericho to make plans to save her family
4. Israel was told to stock food in preparation 7 days before crossing the Jordan into the Promised Land

5. The Shunnamite woman was warned by Elisha of an imminent 7 year famine
6. Israel was promised abundant crops before the land was rested on the Sabbatical years and Jubilee years

By instruction only

These types of preparation were to be made only at specific times and only under specific instruction by the Lord. Hoarding food and wealth in normal times as a substitute for trusting God is not being obedient.

The Lord Jesus Christ has graciously given us a detailed picture in advance of what will happen, what to expect and has promised that He will bring His Church victoriously through the test of the Tribulation.

"But when you see these things begin to take place, straighten up and lift up your heads because your redemption is drawing near." Luke 21:28.

Chapter Eight

The Abomination of Desolation in 2027

Based on the 2030 Return of Jesus Christ, there is good reason to expect the Abomination of Desolation to occur in early 2027. Since the Tribulation will begin sometime after the Day of Pentecost in the summer of 2023, and the Abomination of Desolation is prophesied to occur in the middle of the "week" at 3 ½ years, we can expect the Antichrist to invade Israel, seat himself in the Jerusalem Temple as God and set up his image there within the first few months of 2027.

History's Darkest Hour

The Abomination of Desolation describes the prophecy of the takeover of the Temple in Jerusalem by the Beast, who will seat himself there and display himself as God. Jews living in Judea are specifically warned to flee immediately to the mountains when this occurs. This will lead to a three and a half year period of time known as the Great Tribulation when violence, plagues, and cosmic disasters will devastate the entire planet. A world government will prevail under the dictatorship of the Beast and the False Prophet, who will compel every person to wear a mark on their forehead or hand, and require all to bow down to an image of the Beast under the threat of execution.

"**Therefore when you see the <u>Abomination of Desolation</u> which was spoken of through Daniel the prophet, standing in the holy place (let the reader understand), then those who are in Judea must flee to the mountains. Whoever is on the housetop must not go down to get the things out that are in his house. Whoever is in the field must not turn back to get his cloak. But Woe to those who are pregnant and to those who are nursing babies in those days! But pray that your flight may not be in the winter, or on a Sabbath. For then there will be a great tribulation, such as has not occurred since the beginning of the world until no, nor ever will be. Unless those days had been cut short, no life would have been saved; but for the sake of the elect those days will be cut short.** Matthew 24: 15-22

Let no one in any way deceive you, for it will not come unless the apostasy comes first, and the man of lawlessness is revealed, the son of destruction, who opposes and exalts himself above every so-called god or object of worship, so that <u>he takes his seat in the temple of God, displaying himself as being God</u>. II Thessalonians 2:3-4

He will speak out against the Most High, and wear down the saints of the Highest One, and he will intend to make alterations in times and in law; and they will be given into his hand for <u>a time, times, and half a time.</u> Daniel 7:25

And he will make a firm covenant with the many for <u>one week, but in the middle of the week</u>, he will put a stop to sacrifice and grain offering; and <u>on the wing of abominations will come one who makes desolate</u>, even until a complete destruction, one that is decreed, is poured out on the one who makes desolate. Daniel 9:27

Forces with him will arise, desecrate the sanctuary fortress, and do away with the regular sacrifice. And they will set up the abomination of desolation. Daniel 11:31

From the time the regular sacrifice is abolished and <u>the abomination of desolation</u> is set up, there will be 1,290 days. How blessed is he who keeps waiting and attains to the 1,335 days! Daniel 12:11-12

Satan rules the world through the Beast

The Abomination of Desolation is the defining event of the Tribulation period and marks the date when Satan, embodied in the Antichrist, will declare himself God in the Jerusalem temple to be worshipped by all the world.

But you said in your heart, "I will ascend to heaven; I will raise my throne above the stars of God, and I will sit on the mount of assembly..." Isaiah 14:13

Therefore I have cast you as profane from the mountain of God, And I have destroyed you, O covering cherub. Ezekiel 28:16

The Overpowering Delusion

For this reason God will send among them deluding influence so that they will believe what is false, in order that they may all be judged who did not believe the truth, but took pleasure in wickedness. II Thessalonians 2:11

"...and you will be hated by all because of My name." Luke 21:17. The hatred of the world for Christ and His people will usher in the time of the complete rule of Satan over all government and authority in the world. The delusion will be complete. All those who have rejected Christ will find themselves forced to take the Mark of the Beast and bow down to the image of the Beast.

The Abomination of Desolation sets in motion the invasion of Israel and the Great Tribulation

1. The Antichrist takes over Israel
2. He stops the Temple sacrifices
3. He seats himself in the Temple and declares himself God
4. Those in Judea are to flee to the mountains of southern Jordan
5. The Beast and his allies go on a rampage against the Jews and only 1/3 of Israelis survive
6. With the False Prophet, the Beast institutes the Mark of the Beast and the worship of his image
7. The Great Tribulation comes into full force as the "Time of Jacob's Troubles"
8. The Church will come under intense persecution
9. The Two Witnesses will show up to oppose the Beast and protect Jews and Christians

The Abomination of Desolation requires a Jerusalem Temple

One of the clearest proofs that another Jerusalem Temple will be built is the fact that the Abomination of Desolation cannot take place unless there is another Temple in Jerusalem. Exactly when and how this will take place is still a mystery, but it may have to occur before Daniel's last week begins. With the current political realities of the Dome of the Rock and the Al Aqsa Mosque occupying the Temple Mont, this will take some type of radical change in the power structures of the Middle East to accomplish. Perhaps another war will clear the way for a temple to be rebuilt. The Antichrist himself will likely play a role in the rebuilding of a temple in Jerusalem, perhaps as a peace broker between Israel and the Muslim nations. The seven year "covenant" may include a plan to rebuild the Temple.

Revelation 11:1-2 also describes a Tribulation temple in Jerusalem:

"Get up and measure the temple of God and the alter, and those who worship in it. Leave out the court which is outside the temple and do not measure it, for it has been given to the nations and they will tread underfoot the holy city for forty two months"

Catastrophe for Israel in 2027

The Lord Jesus gives a clear warning for those living in Judea to flee to the mountains when the Abomination of Desolation is set up.

"Therefore when you see the Abomination of Desolation which was spoken of through Daniel the prophet, standing in the holy place (let the reader understand), then those who are in Judea must flee to the mountains... But pray that your flight may not be in the winter, or on a Sabbath. Matthew 24: 15-10.

Two thirds of all Israelis will be killed by the Beast and his allies when he takes over Jerusalem. Only those who heed the Lord's warning to flee to the mountains will survive.

"It will come about in all the land," Declares the Lord, "that two parts in it will be cut off and perish; but the third will be left in it. And I will bring the third part through fire, refine them as silver is refined, and test then as gold is tested. They will call on My Name..."Zechariah 13:7-9.

"Pray that your flight may not be in the <u>winter</u>..." may be an important clue that the Abomination of desolation will indeed happen in winter. The start of the Tribulation and the Second Coming will occur in the summer of 2023 and 2030 respectively., which means that the Abomination must take place in the mid to late winter of 2027.

Chapter Nine

The Seventh Trumpet Rapture

Most Evangelical Christians are taught that Jesus will return secretly and invisibly to gather the Church in the Rapture before the Tribulation. The problem with this theory is that a secret return and invisible rapture cannot be found anywhere in the Bible. In fact neither can a Pre-Tribulation rapture and return be found at all. There is not a single verse of Scripture which states that this will happen. None.

What any student of the Scriptures can find clearly stated and confirmed throughout the Bible is a Rapture after the Tribulation at the sound of the Seventh Trumpet when Jesus appears on the clouds to gather His elect.

The Rapture will occur at the last Trumpet.

Behold, I tell you a mystery, we will not all sleep but we will all be changed, in a moment in the twinkling of an eye, at the <u>last trumpet</u>. I Corinthians 15:51-52.

The Seventh Trumpet is the last trumpet in the Bible.

"Then the seventh angel sounded; and there were loud voices in heaven saying, "The kingdom of the world has become the kingdom of our Lord and His Christ; and He will reign forever and ever." Revelation 11:15.

Jesus states very clearly that His return and the gathering of the elect will happen after the Tribulation, not before.

But immediately <u>after the tribulation</u> of those days…He will send forth His angels with a <u>great trumpet</u> and they will gather together His elect from the four winds, from one end of the sky to the other. Matthew 24: 31.

II Thessalonians 2 places the Lord's return and the Rapture after the antichrist is revealed and the apostasy takes place.

"Now we request you brethren with regard to <u>the coming of our Lord Jesus Christ and our gathering together with Him</u>, that you not be quickly shaken from your composure or be disturbed by either a spirit or a message or a letter as if from us to the effect that the day of the Lord has come. Let no one in any way deceive you, <u>for it will not come unless the apostasy comes first, and the man of lawlessness is revealed</u>, the son of destruction, who opposes and exalts himself above every so-called god, or object of worship, so that he takes his seat in the temple of God, and displays himself as being god." II Thessalonians 2:1-4.

The book of Revelation is clear that the first resurrection will not happen until the antichrist takes over and institutes his mark and the worship of his image which Christians will not bow down to.

"And I saw the souls of those who had been

beheaded because of their testimony of Jesus and because of the Word of God, and those who had not worshipped the beast or his image, and had not received the mark of the beast on their forehead or on their hand; and they came to life and reigned with Christ for a thousand years...**This is the first resurrection**." Revelation 20:4-6.

Paul states in I Thessalonians that the first resurrection will take place just before the Rapture when Jesus Himself descends from heaven.

For the Lord Himself will descend from heaven with a shout, with the voice of the archangel, and the trumpet of God, and the dead in Christ will rise first, then we who are alive and remain will be caught together in the clouds to meet the Lord in the air, and so we shall always be with the Lord. I Thessalonians 4:16-18.

Since there can obviously be only one First Resurrection, these two resurrections are certainly one and the same.

The Mystery of God, which is Christ and the Church (Ephesians 3:1-10 and Colossians 1:26-27,2:2) will be finished at the Seventh Trumpet, not before. It will no longer be a mystery because every eye shall see Him and the Rapture of the Church too.

In the days of the voice of the seventh angel, when he is about to sound, then the mystery of God is finished as He preached to His servants the prophets. Revelation 10:7.

Behold, He is coming on the clouds, and <u>every eye will see Him</u>, even those who pierced Him; and all the tribes of the earth will mourn over Him. Revelation 1:7.

When Christ who is our life is revealed, then <u>you also will be revealed</u> with Him in glory. Colossians 3:4.

The Bible never says the Church will not be here during the Tribulation

Nowhere does the Bible say the Church will not be here during the Tribulation. On the contrary, Jesus said,

"Behold, I have forewarned you."

He commanded us to be alert, prayerful and prepared:

"...for it will come upon all those who dwell on the face of the earth. But keep on the alert at all times, praying that you may have strength to escape all these things that are about to take place, and to stand before the Son of Man." Luke 21:35-36.

The Church is not to fear the Tribulation but to be full of confidence and hope because it is a sure sign that the Lord Jesus will soon appear.

"But when you see these things begin to take place, straighten up and lift you heads, because your redemption is drawing near." Luke 21:28.

Rahab and the Seventh Trumpet Rapture

Prophetic types from the Hebrew Scriptures can give us valuable insight and confirmation about many of the events of the Lord's return. One of the most detailed is the battle of Jericho.

The fortress of Jericho was the first obstacle Israel had to face before they could begin their conquest of Canaan. Joshua sent two men to spy out the city. A prostitute named Rahab hid the two from the king of Jericho in her inn that sat on the wall. Before they made their escape, they told Rahab to hang a red cord from her window so the Israelites would know not to harm her and her family when the city fell.

God told Joshua to have the priests march around the city with the Ark of the Covenant once a day for six days, blowing trumpets on each march. He also instructed them to march around the city seven times on the seventh day, blowing trumpets each time as well. When the seventh trumpet is sounded on the seventh day, the people gave a shout and the walls of Jericho fell down. The city was then put to the sword and Joshua sent the two spies back in to escort Rahab and her family safely out.

This story is a perfect picture of the Seven Seals and Seven Trumpets of Revelation. Just like Rahab is taken out of the city after the seventh trumpet on the seventh day, the Church will be taken out in the Rapture at the Seventh Trumpet of the Seventh Seal of the Tribulation. If the rapture were pre-Tribulation, Rahab as a type of the Church, would have been taken out before the first of the seven days of the battle Jericho. When the seventh trumpet sounded on the seventh day, Israel gave a shout just as the Lord will descend with a shout at the Seventh Trumpet of the Seventh Seal to rapture the Church.

The two angel escort for the rapture

Like the two spies that escort Rahab out of Jericho after the seventh trumpet, two angels escort Lot and his family out of Sodom before it is destroyed. These are a prophetic picture of the Two Witnesses of Revelation 11 who are killed, raised and raptured just before the Seventh Trumpet, providing a kind of escort for the Church at the end of the Tribulation.

The rainbow sign after the Tribulation

After Noah's family and the animals are saved through the flood, God sets a rainbow in the sky as a picture of the return of the Lord after the Tribulation. In Revelation the rainbow makes its appearance just before the Seventh Trumpet, over the head of the Mighty Angel, who is a symbolic representation of Jesus at His return. A rainbow will almost certainly be the Sign of the Son of Man that will be seen in the sky immediately before Jesus appears. The angel also gives a shout, just as there will be a shout when Christ appears.

Elijah's post-Tribulation chariot

Elijah is taken up into heaven in a chariot of fire, as Elisha watches, a prophetic picture of the Rapture of the Church. This happens after a period of terrible Tribulation, the worst Israel had ever experience, a picture that the rapture will occur after the Tribulation.

Crossing the Jordan's Tribulation waters

Israel crossed the flooded Jordan River miraculously on dry ground to enter the Promised Land. The Jordan River is a type of the Tribulation which must be crossed before the Second Coming takes place. David also crossed the Jordan at his own second coming after the defeat of Absalom. Jehu crossed it as well to execute judgment on the enemies of God as a picture of the returning Lion of Judah. Jesus also crossed the Jordan before raising Lazarus, as a prophetic type of His return after the Tribulation.

There is no rainbow, no two witnesses, and no shout prophesied to occur before the beginning of the Tribulation, only at the end, clearly placing the Rapture and Return at the Seventh Trumpet as pictured in the prophetic types, and not before.

A summary of why we can be absolutely sure that the Rapture will happen at the Seventh Trumpet and not before

1. A pre-Tribulation rapture is found nowhere in the Bible. There is not a single verse of Scripture that states this will happen.

2. At least five Scriptures passages clearly, straightforwardly state that the Lord will return to gather us, the elect, <u>after</u> the Tribulation, the Great Apostasy and the Abomination of Desolation: Matthew 24:14-21 & 29-31, Mark 13:24-27, Luke 21:25-28, II Thessalonians 2:1-4 and Daniel 7:21-22.

3. I Corinthians 15:51-52 clearly states that the Rapture will happen at the Last Trumpet. There are seven trumpets sounded at the end of the Tribulation, so a Pre-Tribulation Rapture is an obviously contradiction to a last trumpet Rapture.

4. The prophetic types of the Hebrew Scriptures prove a Seventh Trumpet Rapture. For instance, during the battle of Jericho, Rahab, a prophetic type of the Church, is not taken out until after the seventh trumpet on the seventh day, just as the Church will not be Raptured until the Seventh Trumpet in the seventh year of the Tribulation. The two angels who escort Lot out of Sodom and the rainbow after the flood match exactly the rapture of the Two Witnesses and the appearance of the rainbow just before the Seventh Trumpet sounds in Revelation 11.

5. The Pre-Tribulation position is not based directly on Scripture, but on faulty Dispensational theology and eschatology invented by John Nelson Darby, a nineteenth century cult founder. This has led to the circular reasoning that only Darby's theology is correct, therefore all prophetic Scripture must be filtered through this theology.

6. The invisible return of Christ and the instant disappearance of Christians are complete fabrications of John Darby and taught nowhere in Scripture. The return of the Lord Jesus is only described in the Scriptures as seen across the entire sky and every eye will see Him, never secret, invisible, instant or seen only by believers.

7. Pre-Tribulationists mistakenly call the Tribulation the judgment and wrath of God, but it is described in Scripture only as a time of testing (Revelation 3:10). Only the Seven Bowls of God's Wrath bear that name and will not be poured out until after the Church is raptured at the end of the Tribulation.

8. The Mystery of God, which is Christ and the Church (Ephesians 2:9, Colossians 1:26-27), is finished (no longer a mystery because every eye will see Him) at the Seventh Trumpet (Revelation 10:7). If a Pre-Tribulation Rapture happened, the Mystery of God would be finished then, not at the Seventh Trumpet.

9. Revelation 20 states that the First Resurrection will occur after the mark of the beast and worship of the beast is instituted during the Tribulation. The Apostle Paul described the resurrection of the dead in Christ as

taking place just before the Rapture when the Lord returns (I Thessalonians 4:16, I Corinthians 15, 20,23). Since there can only be one First Resurrection, the Resurrection/Rapture at Christ's coming has to be one and the same as the First Resurrection of Revelation 20.

10. There is not one verse of Scripture that says the Church will not be here during the Tribulation, on the contrary, Jesus commanded us to be alert, prayerful and prepared for the events that are about to come upon the whole world.

Chapter Ten

Deconstructing Darby's Pre-Trib Rapture

The absence from Church history

Before the nineteenth century, Evangelical pastors, scholars and teachers believed that the Second Coming and the rapture of the Church would happen after the Tribulation. It was considered obvious from the Scriptures that the events described in Christ's Olivet Discourse that, **"There will be a great tribulation such has not occurred since the beginning of the world..."** (Matthew 24:21) as well as the rise of the Antichrist and the Abomination of Desolation, will certainly precede the Lord's visible appearance:

"But immediately after the tribulation of those days... they will see the Son of Man coming on the clouds of the sky with power and great glory. And He will send forth His angels with a great trumpet, and they will gather together His elect from the four winds..." Matthew 24:29-31.

There is no evidence that a pre-Tribulation rapture and invisible return of Christ was even discussed among Evangelical pastors or scholars or anyone else before the nineteenth century. None of the reformers like Luther or Calvin and no one else who followed ever taught it or gave any indication that there was such a thing. Even as far back as the so-called Church Fathers, this doctrine was never debated. A few brief mentions from a few obscure writers are often used as proof that it was previously taught in the Church but the meaning of these references are debatable and provide no evidence that this idea was shared by anyone else or discussed at all among any other Biblical scholars.

An elaborate invention by a clever lawyer

Every person who believes that Jesus Christ will return invisibly and that the Church will be gathered up before the Tribulation can trace their belief back to one single individual: John Nelson Darby. Darby was a nineteenth century lawyer, preacher and self-styled theologian. In the 1830's he became part of a British congregation that splintered off from the Church of England called the Plymouth Brethren. Long story short (it would take a book to give this history fair treatment), he invented a system of Biblical theology called Dispensationalism, as well as the pre-Tribulation rapture and invisible return of Christ. as it is widely understood and accepted today. He also invented a long list of dubious interpretations and doctrines associated with the pre-Trib Rapture like the "seven ages of the church," the "non-church tribulation saints," and the "perpetual imminence of the rapture."

Darby became prominent in the Plymouth Brethren, but split off and formed his own group, the Exclusive Brethren, over disagreements about his theology and his authoritarian leadership. He traveled to America where he aggressively pushed his new system of theology and eschatology at a time when interest in Last Days prophecy was exploding in popularity in American Churches.

Scofield Reference: why theology doesn't belong in the Bible

Darby's Dispensational theology and Second Coming eschatology was popularized by Cyrus Scofield who created a commentary Bible in 1909 based on his teachings. The Scofield Reference King James Bible became a required manual for all serious fundamentalist students of the Scriptures. Other Evangelical teachers and preachers like D.L. Moody (the most popular American evangelist of the 19th century) became ardent Dispensationalists.

Also Clarence Larkin, who created a book of illustrations based on Dispensatonalism and Lewis Sperry Chafer who started the Dallas Theological Seminary helped grow the influence of Darby's theology. It eventually spread to most fundamentalist churches and seminaries and came to dominate Evangelical teaching on the Last Days.

Extra-Biblical Dispensationalism

For many Christians, Dispensationalism is the ideal system of theology to explain the Bible and Last Days prophecy. Although it includes many useful facts, principals and ideas, the problem is that it's seven dispensations are never mentioned in the Bible. Only two dispensations are stated: the dispensation of Law and the dispensation of Grace.

The Lord Jesus never taught seven dispensations, the Apostles never taught seven dispensations and the Prophets never taught them either. It is a man-made tool invented to explain a system of theology, not inspired Scripture even though it is often presented as such.

Filtering Prophetic Scripture through faulty theology

The real problem arises when such a faulty and contrived system of theology is used to filter everything in the Scriptures, Last Days prophecy in particular. Instead of beginning with the Bible exclusively and using Scripture to interpret Scripture, Darby's Dispensationalism is applied first by pre-Tribulation teachers and everything else in the Bible must conform to that theological system. So the pre-Tribulation rapture is not based solely and clearly on direct statements of Scripture. It is a kind of back door doctrine. John Nelson Darby's theology and eschatology must be studied and accepted in order to arrive at a pre-Tribulation rapture and invisible Return. No believer today can arrive at a pre-Tribulation Rapture belief by studying the Scriptures alone because it simply isn't there. It must be taught through Darby's theology. The fact remains that there is not one verse in the Bible which says the Second Coming and Rapture will happen this way.

"No prophecy of Scripture is a matter of one's own interpretation, for no prophecy was ever made by an act of human will, but men moved by the Holy Spirit spoke from God." II Peter 1:20.

There is only one correct interpretation of prophetic Scripture: that which God intended. Scripture must interpret Scripture through the Holy Spirit, not through a 19th century cult founder's theology.

Spurgeon and Mueller's warnings

Evangelical ministers of Darby's day warned of the cult-like aspects of Darby's Exclusive Brethren group, where he exercised authoritarian control. Even today the reclusive Exclusive Brethren are considered an extreme cult by most good Evangelical churches; steeped in legalism, authoritarian leadership, and heretical teachings.

Darby was infamous for his rancorous squabbles and condemnations of other Christian leaders who questioned his extreme eschatology and theological inventions, among them George Mueller, highly regarded as a champion of the faith by believers even today. Charles Spurgeon, a contemporary of John Darby and considered by many to be the greatest evangelist and Bible teacher of the 19th century, had little good to say about Darby, his theology or his group. Spurgeon was sharply critical of Darby and his authoritarian cult. He published numerous articles in his news letter about the more unseemly aspects of Darby's ministry such as this one by James Grant:

"In his case it assumes the form of infallibility. Mr. Darby is, to all intents and purposes a thorough Pope, though under a Protestant name. He will never admit that he is in error... how need we feel surprised that Mr. Darby, as the 'prophet, priest, and king' of the party, should exercise a perfect despotism within the domains of Darbyism?. . ."

"Plymouth Brethren have no feeling wherever their principles are concerned. I know indeed of no sect or denomination so utterly devoid of kindness of heart. It is the most selfish religious system with which I am acquainted. It is entirely wrapped up in itself. It recognizes no other denomination, whether the Church of England, or either of the Nonconformist denominations, as a church of Christ. Mr. Darby has again and again said in print, as well as written in private, that those who belong to his party in the metropolis, constitute the only church of Christ in London. . . ." *James Grant, who wrote several articles in Spurgeon's 1869 "Sword and Trowel."*

Spurgeon commented on Grant's article: "Mr. Grant has done real service to the churches by his treatise on "The heresies of the Plymouth Brethren," which we trust he will publish in a separate form. It is almost impossible for even his heavy hand to press too severely upon this malignant power, whose secret but rapid growth is among the darkest signs of the times."

George Mueller, an evangelist who is still well known for his faith-based orphanage ministry was once a member of the Plymouth Brethren. After being condemned by Darby for questioning his theology, he had this to say: "My brother I am a constant reader of the Bible, and I soon found out what I was taught to believe did not always agree with what my Bible said. I came to see I must either part company with what John Darby (said), or my precious Bible, and I chose to cling to my Bible and part from Mr. Darby."

George Mueller also was adamant that II Thessalonians

2 clearly states that a pre-Apostasy/Antichrist coming of Christ will not occur: "The Scripture declares plainly that the Lord Jesus will not come until the apostasy shall have taken place, and the man of sin ... shall have been revealed..." George Mueller.

Pre Tribulation Inventions and Misinterpretations

The list of arguments often used to try to prove the pre-Tribulation Rapture is quite lengthy and can be daunting to untangle. Here are some of the most common types of statements usually given to prove this teaching. They can all be answered by Biblical statements and refuted by sound Biblical arguments.

1. "The Rapture will happen before the Tribulation"

This teaching is found nowhere in the Bible. It is often stated as fact but there is not a single Scripture that says this will happen. What is more, it contradicts straightforward statements of Scripture that describe a Seventh Trumpet, post-Tribulation Rapture. Matthew 24 says the return and Rapture will happen after the Tribulation, I Thessalonians 2 says the Rapture will take place after the Antichrist is revealed, and II Corinthians 15 says the Rapture will happen at the Last Trumpet which is sounded at the end of the Tribulation, not the beginning. See Chapter 2.

2. "The return of Christ will be invisible"

Found nowhere in the Bible. A complete fabrication

without any Scriptural foundation what so ever. The Ascension of Jesus was an entirely visible event witnessed by everyone around Him as it unfolded.

"And after He said these things He was lifted up while they were <u>looking on</u>, and a cloud received Him out of their sight... "This Jesus who has been taken up from you into heaven, will come <u>in just the same way</u> as you have watched Him go into heaven." Acts 1:9-11.

If the return of Jesus Christ must happen in <u>just</u> the same way as He ascended into heaven, it has be a visible, bodily return and certainly cannot be an invisible one. Acts 1:11 contradicts any notion of an invisible return of the Lord as well as all the other many Scriptures describing the Second Coming as an visible event only. See Chapter 10.

3. *"The Rapture will be instant and invisible"*

Not in the Bible anywhere. I Corinthians 15: 51-52 is often cited as proof of this but that passage of Scripture describes only our bodily transformation being instant, not the catching up of believers into the air:

"Behold I tell you a mystery, we will not all sleep but we will all be changed, in a moment, in the twinkling of an eye at the last trumpet; for the trumpet will sound and the dead will be raised imperishable, and we will be changed."

The subject of all 30 verses before this Scripture are entirely about the nature of the bodies we will receive at the Coming of Christ. The actual catching up is not mentioned anywhere in this chapter.

The Bible doesn't teach an invisible Rapture either. This idea contradicts Colossians 3:4 which says: **"When Christ who is our life is <u>revealed,</u> then you will also be <u>revealed</u> with Him in glory."**

How can the Church be revealed at His Coming if the Rapture is invisible?

The prophetic pictures of the Rapture also depict this event as definitively visible and seen by believers as well as unbelievers.

"If you <u>see</u> me when I am taken from you it will be so…" Elijah went up by a whirlwind into heaven, Elijah <u>saw</u> it… II Kings 2:9-12.

After three and a half days the breath of life came into them; and they stood on their feet; and great fear fell on those who were <u>watching</u> them… And they heard a loud voice from heaven saying to them: "Come up here." Then they went up into heaven in a cloud and their enemies <u>watched</u> them. Revelation 11:11-12.

4."The Seven Churches of Revelation are seven ages of the Church"

A complete fabrication. There is nothing in the Bible that says this or even hints at this idea. These seven ages were invented by John Darby because Revelation 2 and 3 posed a problem for his fallacious pre-Tribulation Rapture doctrine. If taken as clearly stated, these letters portray a Church that is being warned and prepared for the approaching Tribulation and return of the Lord.

Unless an alternative interpretation was fabricated, the letters to the Seven Churches would destroy any notion that the Church will not be here during the Apocalypse, hence no pre-Tribulation Rapture either. Interpreting these as seven church ages pulls the Seven Churches back into history instead of on the cusp of the Tribulation; a clever trick to be sure, but contrary to what the Seven Letters actually describe.

The Church age is spoken of in Scripture as one complete age and never more than one. "**And behold I am with you always, even to the end of the age.**" Matthew 21:19. If there were seven church ages, then the Lord would be with us only to the end of the first church age. Absurd of course.

It is safe to say that the Seven Churches of Revelation represent the entire Church body as it will be just before the Second Coming. These letters are really a prophecy of the state of the Church just as the Tribulation period is about to begin.

5. *"Revelation 3:10 says the Church will not go through the Tribulation"*

No, it says the Philadelphia church of first century Asia minor will not be tested. This is one of the most quoted Scriptures as proof that the Church will not go through the Tribulation:

"**I also will keep you** *(the Church in Philadelphia)* **from the hour of testing, that hour which is about to**

come upon the whole world, to test those who dwell on the earth." Revelation 3:10.

This passage is almost always taken out of context by pre-Tribulation advocates. Most quote it without disclosing that it was actually written to the Church in Philadelphia, only one of the seven churches of first century Asia Minor. It is a classic case of cherry picking. Why is only the Church at Philadelphia picked out of these seven to represent the entire last days Church? There is no Scripture that supports this notion at all. In fact all of the Seven Churches are addressed by the Lord as if He will soon return and wants them all to get ready.

There is a context of Christ's impending Appearance as well as the impending Tribulation in all of the letters to the seven churches, not just to the Church in Philadelphia. Most of the Seven are told that they will be going through testing, tribulation or refining.

The Church in Philadelphia is described as having little power:

"Behold, I have put before you a door which no one can shut because you have a little power, and have kept My word, and have not denied My Name." Revelation 3:8.

You could hardly use the words "little power" to describe the Church today. The Philadelphians are part of a larger Last Days Church but they will be spared the test of the Tribulation, probably because they will have already been tested and proven faithful to Jesus.

"...the hour of testing, that hour <u>which is about to come</u> upon the whole world. "

Contrary to proving a pre-Tribulation Rapture this verse actually proves that the letters to the Seven Churches are prophecies about the state of the Church as it will be just before the Tribulation begins, and believers can certainly expect to be here during that time, even if each of the Seven Churches has a distinctive experience.

6. *"John's entrance into heaven is a type of the Rapture"*

Once again the Bible never says this or gives any real reason to believe it. John is taken up into heaven only in spirit, not bodily. But an actual bodily resurrection and rapture does occur in the book of Revelation: that of the Two Witnesses in chapter 11. But pre-Tribulation fans choose to ignore this event even though it precisely matches the Rapture as it is described in the rest of the New Testament, perhaps because it takes place at the end of the seven year Tribulation, not before.

7. *"II Thessalonians 2 says the Rapture will happen before the antichrist is revealed"*

No, II Thessalonians 2 says just the opposite; that the Church will not be gathered up until <u>first</u> the apostasy takes place and the man of sin is revealed.

Now we request you brethren <u>with regard to the coming of our Lord Jesus Christ and our gathering together with Him</u>, that you not be quickly shaken up from you composure or be disturbed either by a

spirit or by a message or a letter as if from us, to the effect that the day of the Lord has come.

Let no one in any way deceive you, for it will not come unless the apostasy comes <u>first</u>, and the man of lawlessness is revealed... II Thessalonians 2: 1-3.

How do you get the Rapture happening before the Antichrist out of that? The whole pre-Tribulation argument hinges on the mistaken notion that the entire Tribulation period is the Day of the Lord, a false claim which Joel completely discredits with his prophesy that the cosmic disasters, identical to those of the sixth seal, will take place <u>before </u>the Day of the Lord (Joel 2:31).

8. *"The Church is not mentioned after Revelation 3 and so is not here"*

Lack of using a particular name does not prove lack of presence. The Church is called by many different names throughout the New Testament: the saints, the brethren, the elect, and these names are all used for believers throughout the book of Revelation. In fact the Great Multitude of gentile believers in Christ from every nation who **"...come out of the Great Tribulation**" (Revelation 7:14), are washed in the blood of the Lamb and follow Him as their Shepherd. This is the perfect definition of the Church even if that particular name is not mentioned.

9. *"Matthew 24 is not for the Church"*

This is a common misinterpretation unsupported by any Scripture. It is strange that all pre-Tribulation teachers say this but then quote verse after verse from Matthew

24 (as well as Mark 13 and Luke 21) to warn Christians today of impending Last Days events.

These chapters are describing the Tribulation period, not anything before. If the Church will be gathered up before these things occur then nothing in these passages have anything to do with the Church.

For instance Luke 21: 28 (**"…straighten up and lift up your heads because your redemption is drawing near"**) is often quoted by pre-Tribulation teachers to encourage believers, but the context occurs during the Tribulation when "**all these things begin to take place.**" If we are taken up before the Tribulation, we won't be here to see any of these things take place because we will be in heaven.

If Matthew 24 is not talking about the Church or written to the Church how can verses like, **"…but of that day and hour no one knows"** and **"…so you too, when you see all these things, recognize that He is near, right at the door"** and **"Therefore be on the alert, for you do not know which day your Lord is coming,"** refer to the Rapture of the Church as routinely taught by pre-Tribulation advocates? Yes they are about the Church so Matthew 24 is certainly speaking about and to the Church. Dismissing the Olivet Discourse just because Dispensationalists say it wasn't written to the Church is unbiblical, bad hermeneutics and dangerous to believers. They want to have their cake and throw it out too.

10. *"The Rapture and Return are always imminent"*

The Bible never calls the Rapture imminent. Suddenness is not imminence. The Rapture will happen suddenly and without warning when it does happen, like a thief in the night. and no man will know the exact day or hour. This doesn't make it perpetually imminent. Imminence means that an event is about to happen. Nothing can be imminent for two thousand years.

"But when you see these things begin to take place straighten up and lift up your heads because <u>your redemption is drawing near</u>." Luke 21:28.

Only when we see "**these things**" of the Tribulation unfolding will we know that the Return of Christ is truly imminent. Until then, "imminent" is not a term that can be used to describe the Return and Rapture before the Tribulation actually begins.

11. *"Absolutely nothing must happen before Jesus returns"*

The Apostle Paul might beg to differ:

...with regard to the coming of our Lord Jesus Christ and our gathering together with Him...Let no one in any way deceive you, <u>for it will not come unless the apostasy comes first, and the man of lawlessness is revealed</u>. II Thessalonians 2:1-3.

Clearly stated by Paul here is the fact that the coming of our Lord Jesus Christ and our gathering together to Him will not come until the apostasy comes <u>first</u> and the man of lawlessness is revealed, exalts himself above all gods and takes his seat in the Temple as God. It just cannot get any more clear than this. This is a simple, straightforward statement of Scripture that the coming of Christ and the Rapture will not take place until the apostasy occurs first and the Antichrist is revealed and seats himself in the Temple to declare himself god. No one has to speculate or read anything into this Scripture; it is stated very plainly.

A list of some of the events that were prophesied to take place before the Appearing and Rapture, contradicting the idea of perpetual imminence:

1. Peter would live into old age (John 21:18)

2. Paul would take the Gospel to the Gentiles (Acts 9:15) and witness in Rome (Acts 23:11)

3. The Church at Smyrna (in 95 A.D.) would have tribulation for ten days (Revelation 2:10)

4. The Gospel would be preached to all the world, (Matthew 24:14, Acts 1:8) which means the whole planet would have to be explored and evangelized, which wasn't completed until the late 20th century.

5. The birth pains of the Tribulation would begin (Matthew 24:8)

6. The Antichrist would appear (Matthew 24:15, II Thessalonians 2:1-4)

7. The Great Apostasy would occur (Matthew 24:10, II Thessalonians 2:1-4)

8 .The world wide persecution of the Church would become severe (Matthew 24:9)

9. The Abomination of Desolation would occur (Matthew 24:15, II Thessalonians 2:1-4)

10. The Temple will have to be rebuilt for the Abomination of Desolation to take place, which means that the Jews would have to be in control of the Temple Mount, which means that the Jews would have to return to the land of Israel and secure sovereignty over Jerusalem (Matthew 24:15), which didn't happen until 1967.

11. Earthquakes, famines, plagues and signs from heaven before the Day of the Lord (Luke 21:11, Joel 2: 30-31)

12. "The Holy Spirit is the Restrainer who will be taken out when the Church is raptured"

Pre-Tribulation teachers are fond of saying this, but the problem is that there is no verse of Scripture that says the Restrainer is the Holy Spirit or the Church. A careful reading of II Thessalonians 2 actually identifies the Restrainer as the Mystery of Iniquity (lawlessness).

The Restrainer does not keep the Antichrist from coming, but keeps him from being revealed, that is, exposed for what he really is; allowing him to deceive the world. It is the "**deception of wickedness**" and "**strong delusion**" the Beast uses "**so that they will believe what is false**."

Paul gives a detailed description of the Restrainer as the

Mystery of Iniquity, reminding the Thessalonians that he had mentioned this source of deception before:

"Do you not remember that while I was still with you I was telling you these things? For <u>the mystery of lawlessness</u> is already at work; only <u>he who now restrains</u> will do so until he is taken out of the way. Then that lawless one will be revealed whom the Lord will slay with the breath of His mouth and bring to an end by the appearance of His coming." II Thessalonians 2:6-8.

Just as Paul said, he spoke of this restraining deception before, such as in II Corinthians 4:4: **"The god of this world has blinded the minds of the unbelievers…"** The Restrainer is neither the Holy Spirit nor the Church so this fails as evidence for a pre-Tribulation Rapture.

13. *"The Tribulation is the Day of the Lord"*

Pure invention. Nowhere in the Bible is the Tribulation called the Day of the Lord. This is based on circular reasoning: since the Rapture must happen before the Day of the Lord, then the Tribulation must be the Day of the Lord. The prophet Joel places the Day of the Lord <u>after</u> the same cosmic events described in the Sixth Seal, which means the Day of the Lord definitely will not happen before the end of the Tribulation.

"The sun will be turned to darkness and the moon into blood <u>before </u>the great and awesome <u>day of the Lord</u>." Joel 2:31.

"I looked when He broke the sixth seal and there was an earthquake, and the sun became black as

sackcloth and the whole moon became like blood..." Revelation 6:12.

The Day of the Lord begins when Jesus Christ shows up. He is clear that this Day will happen **"...immediately after the tribulation of those days...they will see the Son of Man coming on the clouds..."** (Matthew 24:29-30). After means after.

14."The prophetic types of the Hebrew Scriptures show a pre-Tribulation Rapture"

Only a short shrift of the prophetic types in the Hebrew Scriptures could support a pre-Tribulation Rapture. For instance, the battle of Jericho and the removal of Rahab before its destruction is sited as proof of the pre-Tribulation Rapture but the fact that she is not taken out until the seventh trumpet on the seventh day is completely ignored. The seven daily marches and the seven trumpets on the seventh day paint a perfect picture of the Seals and Trumpets of Revelation but Rahab's Seventh Trumpet gathering up is never mentioned by pre-Tribulation advocates. This wonderful story pictures a Seventh Trumpet Rapture and only a Seventh Trumpet Rapture.

The story of Lot is another example given as pre-Trib proof, but the importance of the two angels as prophetic types of the Two Witnesses who will appear at the end of the Tribulation, is completely overlooked as well. The destruction of Sodom and the conquest of Jericho are both types of the Seven Bowls of Wrath, not the Seven Seals and Seven Trumpets of the Tribulation period.

15. "Only a pre-Tribulation Rapture can account for a two part coming of Christ"

The Second Coming of Jesus will happen in two parts: the Appearance on the Clouds and the White Horse Return. The first part is to gather the Church and the second part is to restore Israel. In between these two events will occur the wedding of the Lamb in heaven and the Bowls of Wrath. Many post-Tribulation advocates get this wrong and try to squeeze the Coming of the Lord into a single event. This is really a separate issue and not evidence against a Seventh Trumpet Rapture.

16. "The Tribulation is the wrath and judgment of God"

This would mean that the Great Multitude of gentile Christians who come out of the Great Tribulation (Revelation 7:14) would be under the wrath and judgment of God. I Thessalonians 5:9 says, **"For God has not destined us for wrath but for obtaining salvation through our Lord Jesus Christ."**

The Tribulation is called a test (Revelation 3:10) but it is never called wrath or judgment in the Scriptures. After the cosmic disasters of the Sixth Seal, the wicked say to the mountains and rocks:

"Fall on us and hide us from the presence of Him who sits on the throne and from the wrath of the Lamb, for <u>the great day of Their wrath has come</u> and who is able to stand?"

This is at the end of the Tribulation. This day of wrath

and the appearance of the Lamb which follow the cosmic disasters of the Sixth Seal are the same disasters that are described by Jesus in Matthew 24 after the Tribulation and just before He comes to gather the elect from the four winds. The wrath of God starts when Christ appears on the clouds, terrifying the followers of the Beast at the end of the Tribulation.

17. "Jesus "initiates" the Seven Seals so they must be the wrath of God"

The breaking of the seals gives permission for testing just as God gave satan permission to test Job. All authority rests in the hands of Jesus Christ. God frequently uses the works of satan to test us, but only as far as the Lord allows. All of the Seals and Trumpets are directly caused by evil men or satan himself, except the Seventh Trumpet, which finishes the Mystery of God *(the Church age)* and officially brings in the Kingdom of God on earth at Christ's Return (Revelation 11:15). The Seven Bowls of God's Wrath are the only plagues that are called wrath because they are the only ones that come directly from the hand of God. The Church will be in heaven for the wedding of the Lamb when the Bowls of Wrath are poured out.

18. "The Great Multitude are not the Church but 'Tribulation Saints'"

Pre-Tribulation proponents insist the Great Multitude of Revelation 7 who come out of the Tribulation from every nation are not the Church. They refer to them only as the "Tribulation Saints" but they are obviously gentile believers in Christ who are **"...washed in the**

blood of the Lamb," and follow Him as their Shepherd. This description exactly fits the Church by whatever name you choose to call them.

Dispensationalists are going into unbiblical territory and flirting with heresy here because there is nothing at all in the Scriptures that makes room for such a separate group of gentile believers. As far as God's people are defined, there is only Israel and the Church. Reference to such a third group cannot be found anywhere in the Bible. "**There is one body and one Spirit...**" Ephesians 4:4. We know Israel is going to be restored after the Church age. "**A partial hardening has happened to Israel until the fullness of the Gentiles comes in, and so all Israel will be saved**." Romans 11:25-26, but a vast para-church gentile body of believers has no basis in Scripture. It is obviously another fabrication of John Darby to prop up his pre-Tribulation Rapture.

They also tell us that Christ would never allow His Bride to go through the Tribulation, but what about the Great Multitude? Is God pouring his wrath on these vast number of gentile believers in Christ? Are they some kind of second class Christians? Are they being punished for being "left behind"? The Great Multitude is certainly the Church. If it looks like a duck...

19. "The pre-Tribulation Rapture is so popular it must be true"

It is surprising how often the popularity card is played in pre-Tribulation circles but this is wholly unbiblical and obviously in error. Since when is prophetic doctrine or any other doctrine correct because of popularity?

74

Salvation by faith alone wasn't very popular either when Martin Luther started preaching it. The Word of God is the only basis for prophetic truth, period.

"...learn not to go beyond what is written." I Corinthians 4:6.

20. *"The Last Trumpet is not the Seventh Trumpet of Revelation"*

This argument is used over and over again by pre-Tribulation teachers but this contradiction to what the Bible actually says is so obvious it is puzzling how anyone could believe it. Read the book of Revelation: there are absolutely no other trumpets mentioned after the Seventh Trumpet. It is the last trumpet in the Bible, not to mention the other obvious fact that a pre-Tribulation rapture trumpet could not honestly be called the last trumpet with seven more trumpets to sound!

If the Last Trumpet is not the Seventh Trumpet, then which number is it; the third or the ninth or the hundredth? By definition, the term "last trumpet" demands that there are previous trumpets. We know that God completes His purposes in sevens, especially in the Apocalypse, so the Last Trumpet really cannot be any other than the Seventh Trumpet. When was Rahab taken out of Jericho, before any of the trumpets were sounded or after the seventh trumpet on the seventh day?

21. "The 144,000 are evangelists who convert the Great Multitude"

No, the Bible never calls them evangelists or ever describes them doing evangelism. These are young Jewish Christians. The Great Multitude will evangelize the 144,000 and bring them to Christ, not the other way around.

The 144,000 are the final stone, the keystone of the building that is the Church (Ephesians 2:20-21). They also provide the direct link between Israel and the Church, the legal representation of every tribe of Israel so that the final redemption of the Jewish nation can go forward.

The story of Joseph is the best way to understand the role that the 144,000 play in the Tribulation period. Joseph's brother Benjamin proves to be the key to the redemption of Israel then, just as the appearance of the 144,000 will be the key to Israel's redemption. Joseph would not reveal himself to his brothers until Benjamin was present, just as Jesus Christ will not reveal Himself to Israel until the 144,000 Jewish Christians out of every tribe of Israel are present.

22. "The Mystery of God is _____ (fill in the blank)"

Pre-Tribulation teachers seem to be completely confused about exactly what is the Mystery of God. The mighty angel of Revelation 10 declares that the Mystery of God will be finished at the Seventh Trumpet:

"...there will be delay no longer, but in the days of

the voice of the seventh angel, when he is about to sound, <u>then the mystery of God is finished</u> as he preached to His servants the prophets." Revelation 10: 6-7.

It seems there are as many interpretations of this verse as there are commentaries on it among pre-Tribulation advocates. Some of the many interpretations of the Mystery of God:

"Everything on God's prophetic schedule of events"

"The culmination of the conflict of the ages"

"Those counsels made known...through the Old Testament prophets"

"When Jesus reveals Himself to the Christians in heaven"

"The destruction of the beast...by the removal of the dragon"

"When the end would come"

"The divine purpose concerning the destiny of the world..."

The Biblical definition of the Mystery of God can be found in Ephesians and Colossians:

"...by revelation there was made known to me the mystery...my insight into <u>the mystery of Christ</u> which in other generations was not made known to the sons of men...<u>the mystery which has for ages been hidden in God</u>...might now be made known

through the church..." Ephesians 3:2-10.

"This <u>mystery</u> is great, but I am speaking with reference to <u>Christ and the church</u>." Ephesians 4:23.

"...the <u>mystery</u> which has been hidden from the past ages and generations, but now has been manifested to His saints, to which God willed to make known what is the riches of the glory of this mystery among the Gentiles, <u>which is Christ in you the hope of glory</u>. ...a true knowledge of God's mystery, that is, Christ Himself.** " Colossians 1:20-22 and 2:2.

Simply stated, the Mystery of God of Revelation 10 is Christ and the Church as preached by the Prophets. It is a mystery because the World at large remains blind to the Gospel and the New Birth, even though it has been preached to all nations.

Revelation 10 describes the Mystery of God as that was **"...preached to His servants the prophets."**

Paul also tells us this mystery was preached by the prophets:

"...according to my gospel and the preaching of Jesus Christ, according to the revelation of <u>the mystery</u> which has been kept secret for long ages past, is now manifested, and <u>by the Scriptures of the prophets</u>, according to the commandment of the eternal God, has been made known to all the nations." Romans 16:25-26.

The Biblical definition of the Mystery of God in Revelation 10 poses a problem for the pre-Tribulation

Rapture doctrine. If the Mystery of God, being Christ in the Church, is not finished until the Seventh Trumpet, then the Church would certainly have to be here until the end of the Tribulation. At that time it would then be a mystery no longer because every eye will see Him and see the rapture of the Church as well.

23. *"The Lord would never allow His Bride to go through the Tribulation"*

Or more crudely: "The Lord would not allow His Bride to get beat up (by the Tribulation)." This is a common statement by pre-Tribulation teachers but it begs the question that the Tribulation is not a time of testing, which it certainly is (Revelation 3:10). It also ignores the fact that the Church is told throughout the New Testament that they will go through tribulation and testing (I Peter 1:6-7) and history has proven this true again and again. So it is ridiculous to ever say that the Church is not supposed to go through tribulation.

The most disturbing aspect of this false notion is that it assumes that the Lord would be wrong to "allow His Bride to go through the Tribulation." By this logic, if you are a pre-Tribulation believer and find yourself in the Tribulation, you would have to assume that the Lord was wrong or uncaring because He allowed you to get "beat up" during the Seven Seals.

Are we Last Days saints better than Paul or James or Stephan and all the other believers down through the centuries who suffered persecutions and tribulations and testing and even death because of their faith? Weren't they the Bride of Christ as much as we are?

It's a test, not wrath or judgment or punishment. Just like Daniel's three friends were brought safely through the fiery furnace, the Lord Jesus will bring His Bride safely through the Tribulation period.

Chapter Eleven

The Invisible Return Heresy

In light of the fact that the Lord Jesus Himself made very clear statements describing His return as a visibly spectacular event, seen from one end of the sky to the other, as well as warning believers not be fooled by anyone teaching a secret return, it is bizarre that any born-again believer would ever accept such a thing. But that is exactly what is has happened. In fact, thanks to Darby's pre-Tribulation eschatology, most Evangelical churches and ministries today, representing many millions of saints, teach that very same false doctrine, even though no one can quote a single Scripture to support it.

Given the Lord's emphasis on His visible return on the clouds as well as the way it is described in Paul's letters and John's Revelation, this must be considered a major doctrinal heresy. It certainly is not a salvation issue or an orthodoxy heresy, but it is a major one nonetheless. False Christian cults and sects often teach that the Lord has returned or will return secretly or invisibly to dupe their ignorant, indiscriminating followers into swallowing their failed and false prophecies. Jesus obviously foresaw this deception by the false teachers of the Last Days and strongly warned us about it.

"For false Christs and false prophets will arise and will show great signs and wonders so as to mislead, if possible even the elect... For just as the lightning comes from the east and <u>flashes</u> *(phainetai: is seen or appears)* **even to the west, so will the coming of the Son of Man be."** Matthew 24: 24,27.

There is Scripture after Scripture which describes in detail the Lord Jesus Himself appearing visibly in the sky to be seen by every person on the planet when He returns. There is not a single verse of Scripture which says or even gives a hint that His return will be secret or invisible or that only believers will see Him. The invisible return is an unbiblical fabrication and must be rejected as a false doctrine and a harmful heresy by anyone who is serious about basing their beliefs exclusively on what the Bible actually says and not on the fabricated doctrines of men.

The Scriptures describing the Rapture and Return specify a visible appearance of Christ only

1. **...looking for that blessed hope and the <u>APPEARING</u> of the glory of our great God and Savior, Christ Jesus.** Titus 2:13

2. **That you keep the commandment without stain or reproach until the <u>APPEARING</u> of our Lord Jesus**

Christ, which He will bring about at the proper time. I Timothy 6:14

3. **Regarding the coming of our Lord Jesus Christ and our gathering together with Him…Then that lawless one will be revealed whom the Lord will slay… by the <u>APPEARANCE</u> of His coming.** II Thessalonians 2:1-8

4. **We know that when He <u>APPEARS</u> we will be like Him, because we will <u>SEE</u> Him just as He is.** I John 3:2.

5. **…Of the glory that is to be <u>REVEALED</u>…and when the Chief Shepherd <u>APPEARS</u>, you will receive the unfading crown of glory.** I Peter 5:1-4

6. **And give relief to you who are afflicted and to us as well when Lord Jesus will be <u>REVEALED FROM HEAVEN WITH HIS MIGHTY ANGELS IN FLAMING FIRE</u>…when He comes to be glorified in His saints on that day, and to be marveled at among all who have believed.** II Thessalonians 1:7-10

7. **When Christ who is our life is <u>REVEALED</u>, then you will also be <u>REVEALED</u> with Him in glory.** Colossians 3:4

8. **..as happened in the days of Lot…It will be just the same on the day that the Son of Man is <u>REVEALED</u>.** Luke 17:26, 30.

9. **So that the proof of your faith, being more precious than gold which is perishable, even though**

tested by fire, may be found to result in praise and glory and honor at the **REVELATION** of Jesus Christ. I Peter 1:7

10. Fix your hope completely on the grace to be brought to you at the **REVELATION** of Jesus Christ. I Peter 1:13

11. Beloved, do not be surprised at the fiery ordeal among you, which comes upon your testing...keep on rejoicing, so that also at the **REVELATION** of His glory you may rejoice with exultation. I Peter 4:12-13

12. Behold He is coming on the clouds and **EVERY EYE WILL SEE HIM** Revelation1:7

13. "But immediately after the tribulaton...they will **SEE** the Son of Man coming on the clouds of the sky with great power and great glory. And He will send forth His angels with a great trumpet and they will gather together His elect from the four winds, from one end of the sky to the other." Matthew 24:31

14. "...after...the Tribulation...they will **SEE** the Son of Man coming in clouds...and will gather His elect..." Mark 13:24-27

15. "Then they will **SEE** the Son of Man coming in a cloud with great power and great glory. But when you see these things begin to take place, straighten up and lift up you heads, because you redemption is drawing near." Luke 21:27-28

16. For <u>THE LORD HIMSELF</u> will descend from heaven with a shout, with the voice of the archangel and with the trumpet of God, and the dead in Christ will rise first. Then we who are alive and remain will be caught up together with them in the clouds to met the Lord in the air. I Thessalonians 4:13-17

Where is an invisible return spoken of in these verses or any other verses of the Bible?

A visible, bodily Ascension can only mean a visible, bodily Return

He was lifted up while they were <u>looking on</u>, and a cloud received Him out of their sight..." This Jesus who has been taken up from you into heaven, <u>will come in just the same way as you have watched Him go into heaven</u>." Acts 1:9-11

How can Jesus <u>Himself</u> return and still be invisible since He has a physical body? He did not ascend into the clouds invisibly but bodily and because the Word of God clearly states that He will return in just the same way, He certainly will not return secretly or invisibly.

The wicked, not just believers will see Him

Christ told those who hated Him that even they will see Him when He comes.

" '...hereafter you will <u>SEE</u> the Son of Man sitting at the right hand of Power, and coming on the

clouds of heaven.' ...Then they spat in His face and beat Him with their fists..." Matthew 26:64, 67.

The prophetic pictures of the Rapture also depict this event as definitively visible and watched by both believers and unbelievers

"If you <u>see</u> me when I am taken from you it *(Elisha's request for a double portion of his spirit)*will be so." ...Elijah went up by a whirlwind into heaven. Elisha <u>saw</u> it... II Kings 2:9-12

After three and a half days the breath of life from God came into them, and they stood on their feet; and great fear fell upon those who were <u>watching</u> them. And they heard a loud voice from heaven saying to them, "Come up here." Then they went up into heaven in a cloud <u>and their enemies watched them</u>. Revelation 11:11-12

The Lord made a point of warning us not to expect His Coming to be hidden or secret but seen across the entire sky

"Behold I have told you in advance. So if they say to you, 'Behold He is in the wilderness,' do not go out, or, 'Behold, He is in the inner rooms,' do not believe them. For just as the lightning comes from the east and flashes *(phainetai: is seen)* even to the west, so will the coming of the Son of Man be." Matthew 24:27

The Lord adamantly taught that His Return will be a visibly spectacular event to warn against false teachers, false prophets, sects and cults that often teach an invisible, secret or false return of Christ.

"See to it that no one misleads you. For many will come in My name, saying, 'I am the Christ,' and will mislead many." Matthew 24:4-5

The true identity of the Church will also be revealed to all the world when the Lord appears on the clouds

When Christ who is our life is revealed, then <u>you will also be revealed</u> with Him in glory. Colossians 3:4

This direct statement of Scripture contradicts the popular depiction of the Rapture as being instantaneous and invisible without the world realizing what happened to all the Christians. The mystery of who God's people really are will be revealed to all the world because every eye will see the Resurrection/Rapture as it unfolds at the Lord's Appearance.

The Scriptures make it clear that the Rapture will occur at the Last Trumpet at the end of the seven year Tribulation

Behold I tell you a mystery, we will not all sleep, but we will all be changed, in a moment, in the twinkling of an eye, <u>at the last trumpet</u>; for the trumpet will

sound, and the dead will be raised imperishable, and we will be changed. I Corinthians 15:51

The Lord completes His purposes in sevens. The Last Trumpet cannot be any other than the Seventh Trumpet. The Seventh Trumpet of Revelation 11 is the last trumpet mentioned in all the Bible.

"But in the days of the voice of the seventh angel, when he is about to sound, then the mystery of God *(Christ and the Church)* **is finished (***no longer a mystery because every eye will see the Appearance/Rapture)***, as He preached to His servants the prophets."** Revelation 10:7

The Lord Jesus Christ will return to reveal Himself to all the world and resurrect the dead in Christ and rapture us believers who are alive; visibly, gloriously, loudly, on the clouds in flaming fire with His mighty angels when the Seventh Trumpet sounds at the end of the Tribulation.

Chapter Twelve

The Meaning of the Seven Seal Scroll

The meaning of the Seven Seals Scroll is one of the most debated questions about the book of Revelation. Many interpret the Scroll as a title deed, while others believe that it is a will or secret prophecies, or a book of judgments or something else.

The Scroll has seven seals which Jesus Christ opens one by one and each seal in turn unleashes some terrible event on the world: conquest, war, famine, death, persecution and cosmic disasters. A subset of seven trumpet plagues then occurs when the Seventh Seal is broken. The opening of the Seven Seals parallels the events that Jesus described as, "**the tribulation of those days**" in Matthew 24. It is also commonly associated with Daniel's seventieth "week."

"The Revelation of Jesus Christ..."

This first phrase of the Apocalypse of John is the theme and narrative of the book of Revelation. The unveiling of Jesus Christ to the world and all the events that lead up to this unveiling and all the events that result from this unveiling is what the last book of the Bible is all about. This apocalypse *(to unveil)* is also what the Scroll with Seven Seals is about.

None but the Lamb is found worthy to break the Seals

In Revelation 5 the Great Commission is completed as the fullness of the Gentiles has come in (Romans 11:25). Christ has accomplished His goal of creating a kingdom of believers from all nations: "**Worthy are you to take the Book and to break its seals; for you were slain and purchased for God with your blood men from every tribe and tongue and people and nation. You have made them to be a kingdom and priests to our God; and they will reign upon the earth.**" Revelation 5:9-10.

The key which unlocks the meaning of the Scroll: the Seventh Trumpet

The breaking of the Scroll's Seven Seals is completed with the Seventh Trumpet of the Seventh Seal. It's contents are then revealed, and it is this moment which can tell us the meaning of the Scroll with Seven Seals. Just before the Seventh Trumpet is sounded, another mighty angel declares: "**There will be delay no longer, but in the days of the voice of the seventh angel, when he is about to sound, then the mystery of God is finished, as He preached** (*gave, announced, declared*) **to His servants the prophets.**" Revelation 10:7.

The breaking of all the seals and the opening of the Scroll finishes the mystery of God which He declared to the prophets. **The Mystery of God as given to the** prophets is the meaning of the Scroll with Seven Seals.

The Seven Seal Scroll is the Mystery of God hidden in the writings of the prophets

We solved one mystery with another mystery. Now we have to solve that one. The Mystery of God is another of those Revelation enigmas that there a lot of debate on and little broad agreement about among Evangelicals. Despite such disagreement, the Mystery of God is no mystery, at least to born-again believers.

The Apostle Paul explains the Mystery of God very clearly in his letters:
"When you read you can understand my insight into <u>the mystery of Christ</u>, which in other generations was not made known to the sons of men. ...<u>the mystery which has for ages been hidden in God</u>." Ephesians 3:4,5,9.

"This <u>mystery</u> is great, but I am speaking with reference to <u>Christ and the Church</u>." Ephesians 5:32.

"The <u>mystery</u> which has been hidden from the past ages and generations ...<u>which is Christ in you the hope of glory</u>." Colossians 1:26,27.

"Now to Him who is able to establish you according to my gospel and the preaching of <u>Jesus Christ according to the revelation of the mystery</u> which has been kept secret for long ages past, but is manifested. and <u>by the Scriptures of the prophets,</u>

according to the commandment of the eternal God, has been made known to all nations..." Romans 16:25-26.

In summary, the Mystery of God is:
1. Jesus Christ
2. The Church (Christ in us)
3. Hidden in ages past
4. Written of in the Scriptures of the Prophets
5. Unveiled to those who turn to Christ and are born-again

The Mighty Angel says the Mystery of God was declared by the prophets. Paul says the mystery of Jesus Christ was made known by the Scriptures of the prophets.

The Mystery of God is Christ and the Church

With this we can solve the meaning of the Scroll. **In short, the Scroll with Seven Seals is the writings of the prophets which declare the Mystery of God, which is Christ and the Church**. At the sounding of the Seventh Trumpet Jesus Christ and the Church will be revealed to every eye and so the Mystery of God which was hidden for ages will be finished, no longer a mystery: "**Behold, He is coming with the clouds and <u>every eye</u> will see Him,,,**" Revelation 1:7.

The Mystery of God is veiled to the World but revealed to believers

"But we speak God's wisdom in a <u>mystery</u>,,, the wisdom which none of the rulers of this age has understood... For <u>to us God revealed them</u>through the Spirit..." I Corinthians 2:7,10.

"But to this day whenever Moses is read, a veil lies over their heart; but whenever a person turns to the Lord <u>the veil is taken away</u>." II Corinthians 4:15.

"For judgment I have come into the world so that those who do not see may see, and those who see may become blind." John 9:39.

There are three phases of the Mystery of God:

1. The Mystery hidden from ages past, written in the Prophets which no one in Old Testament times really understood
2. The Mystery preached by Christ and the Apostles which only born-again believers can understand through the Holy Spirit
3. The Mystery written in the Seven Seal Scroll which at the Seventh Trumpet will be unveiled to all the world at Christ's appearance, but the vast majority of mankind will have the mark of the beast and so cannot repent

Written on the Seven Seal Scroll are the prophetic Scriptures about Christ and the Church, the Mystery of God

Daniel was told, **"But as for you Daniel, conceal these words and <u>seal up the book</u> until the end of time** *(or time of the end).***"** Daniel 12:4. Daniel's prophesies about Jesus Christ are part of that Scroll with Seven Seals which has been sealed until the time of the end when the Lord breaks the seals and then unveils the Mystery for all the world to see. All the other writing of the Hebrew prophets from Moses to Malachi which spoke of Christ and the Church in parables, symbols and prophecies are represented in the Seven Seal Scroll as well.

The Seals of the Scroll

The Seals are not the opening of the Scroll, **the seals are the prerequisite which must be met before the contents of the Scroll can be unveiled**. The Seven Seals are a test: **"...to test those who dwell on the earth."** Revelation 3:10. They are not wrath or judgment or the Day of the Lord. The catastrophes of the Seals come from Satan and the Beast, not from God. They are a test of the loyalties of everyone in the world, but especially of the Church.

The Lord appeared after Daniel's friends were tested

Hananiah, Michael and Azariah were put to the test when the king of Babylon commanded all the world to bow down and worship the golden image. They refused and so were thrown into the fiery furnace. As the king looked into the flames, he saw a fourth man and said **"...the appearance of the fourth is like the son of the**

gods!" Daniel 3:25. Nebuchadnezzer saw the Lord in the flames and realized that the God of Daniel's friends was the true God. The three walked out of the fiery furnace but those who threw them in were killed. The furnace was heated seven times hotter, marking it as a type of the Seven Seal Tribulation.

The Lord appeared after Job was tested

The story of Job is a prophetic picture of the Tribulation period as well. Job is tested by various catastrophic plagues of Satan while his friends challenge the genuineness of his faith. In the end God appears and reveals Himself as El Shaddai, God Almighty, the Creator of the heavens and the earth. Job is restored with greater riches than He had before while his friends come under judgment. Just as God gave Satan permission to test Job, the Lamb in opening the seals, will give Satan permission to test the whole world by the events of the Tribulation.

The Lord will appear after the Church is tested

The Seven Seals of the Tribulation is a test to show who is the true Lord of the Universe and who are God's true people. The whole world will be put to the test to prove that Jesus is Lord and the Church are the true people of God, not the followers of the Beast or any other faith.

The Test on Mt Carmel

The test on Mt Carmel is also a prophetic picture of the test of the Seven Seals of the Tribulation. During the reign the wicked king Ahab and his Baal worshipping wife Jezebel, Israel was devastated by drought, famine, persecutions, apostasy, murder, tyranny and idolatry. The prophet Elijah proposed a test of two sacrificial alters to see who's god would show up to light the sacrifice: Baal or Jehovah. The 450 prophets of Baal pleaded all day, even cutting themselves with no results. Elijah then repaired the broken alter of Israel, put the sacrifice on it, and even poured water over it three times. He then called on the Lord and fire fell from heaven and burned up the sacrifice and the entire alter as well. In the test on Mount Carmel, the prophets of Baal were defeated and the Lord revealed Himself to Israel as the One True God.

"When the people saw it they fell on their faces; and they said, 'The Lord He is God; the Lord, He is God." I Kings 18:39.

During the test of the Tribulation, the Kingdom of the World under the Antichrist will be defeated and Jesus Christ will reveal Himself as the One True Lord.

"...at the name of Jesus every knee will bow...and that every tongue will confess that Jesus Christ is Lord..." Philippians 2:10-11.

The Lord will bring the Church safely through the Tribulation while those who worship the statue of the

Beast and wear his mark will be destroyed. Then will Jesus Christ appear on the clouds at the Seventh Trumpet to rapture the Church. Everyone, even the followers of the Beast, will see with their own eyes that Jesus Christ is the Creator of the universe and born-again Christians are His people; realizing in the process that they about to be judged: **"And they said to the mountains and to the rocks, 'fall on us and hide us from the One who sits on the throne and from the wrath of the Lamb; for the great day of Their wrath has come and who is able to stand?'"** Revelation 6:16-17.

The beast and his followers will fail the test

Daniel passed the test of the lion's den and was promoted. His three friends passed the test of the fiery furnace and were promoted. The king of Babylon was weighed in the scales and found wanting in the famous writing on the wall:

"'MENE – God has numbered your kingdom and put an end to it. 'TEKEL' – you have been weighed in the scales and found deficient. 'PERES' – your kingdom has been divided and given over to the Medes and Persians." Daniel 5: 26-27.

The beast and his followers will fail the test of the Seven Seals, lose the kingdom of the world and come under the judgment of the Seven Golden Bowls of Wrath.

Christ will make His Church victorious in the Tribulation

The Church that the Lord Jesus bought with His own blood out of every nation will emerge victorious from the Tribulation: **"And they overcame him** *(the dragon)* **because of the blood of the Lamb ad because of the world of their testimony, and they did not love their lives even when faced with death. ...those who had been victorious over the beast and his image and the number of his name..."** Revelation 12:11, 15:2.

Chapter Thirteen

The Seven Churches of the Last Days

The biggest mistake many prophecy "experts" make about the Seven Churches of Revelation is teaching that they represent seven ages of the Church. This is a false teaching and a complete fabrication by John Nelson Darby without any evidence to support it from anywhere in the Bible. The Church age is spoken of in the Scriptures only as one complete age and never as more than one.

"And lo I am with you always, even to the end of the *(Church)* **age."** Matthew 28:19.

A problem for the Pre-Tribulation Rapture

The seven ages were invented by Darby because these particular Scriptures posed a problem for his fallacious Pre-Tribulation Rapture doctrine. If taken as clearly stated, these letters portray a Church that is being warned and prepared for the test of the approaching Tribulation period. Unless an alternative interpretation was fabricated, the letters to the Seven Churches would destroy any notion that the Church will not be here during the Apocalypse, hence no Pre-Trib rapture either. Interpreting these as seven church ages pulls the Seven Churches back into history instead of on the cusp of the Tribulation. A clever trick, to be sure, but wholly unbiblical and contradictory to what the Seven Letters actually describe.

Free to understand the real message of the Seven Letters

The problem with this false teaching is that it corrupts and hides the true purpose of these seven letters to the Seven Churches of Revelation. Many believers have been confused by Darby's teaching on this and so don't realize what the Lord Jesus really wants to teach us here. The lessons we need to understand from these seven letters is of vital importance to the Church as we approach the Tribulation period.

Much like a "State of the Union" Speech

The Seven Letters could be described as a "State of the Church" message. In these letters the Lord is telling us as the Church (or churches) where we stand at this time in history and what we need to do to become spiritually prepared for His Return. The Letters to the Seven Churches are prophecies about the End Times Church. The same way John the Baptist was sent to prepare Israel for Christ's first coming, these letters were written to the Church of the Last Days to prepare us for His second coming.

Christ's immediate Return is declared to the Seven Churches

The Lord makes it very clear to all Seven Churches that He is about to return:
"I am coming to you"..."I am coming to you quickly"..."hold fast until I come"..."you will not know what hour I will come to you"..."I am coming quickly"..."I stand at the door." This is the true definition of imminence, that one short period just before the Tribulation begins, not the false definition that supposedly has gone on for 2,000 years according to the pre-Tribulation theory.

Revelation was written to End Times believers more than anyone else

It is clear that the Lord is writing to these seven churches as if they were all about to go into the Tribulation period. In fact the whole of the book of Revelation is presented in this "futurity" literary style, as if John were seeing it all take place right then. Much like the book of Daniel, Revelation has apparently been **"concealed and sealed up"** until the End Times (Daniel 12:9), that is, a fully accurate understanding of it would be given only to those believers who would be here when it all occurred. This is why Revelation has been the most misunderstood and misinterpreted book in the Bible.

The Apostles were told of the Lord's Return, **"It is not for you to know times or epochs which the Father**

has fixed by His own authority." Acts 1:7. This makes perfect sense because first century believers did not have to prepare for the Tribulation because it wouldn't happen for another 2,000 years. The Church through the centuries didn't have to understand the times of the Apocalypse but we do. We are the generation that this will all happen to. Like giving a passenger their ticket just before the plane departs, a full and accurate understanding of Revelation is now being disclosed to believers that past generations were not privileged to see.

Only those who heed the words of Revelation will be blessed

"And behold I am coming quickly. Blessed is he who <u>heeds</u> the words of the prophecy of this book." Revelation 22:7.

The prophecy "experts" who continue to reject Christ's warnings to the churches to prepare them for the approaching Apocalypse will remain in a state of confusion about this book. Only those who actually **heed** the Revelation of John will understand it fully and be blessed by it. Those who brush it aside by denying the Church will be here during the Tribulation will be dangerously unprepared. They will easily fall victim to the Antichrist and will not live to see the day of Christ's return. Just as those who do not **heed** the warnings of an approaching storm are the ones who will be its victims. The people of Noah's day did not heed his warnings and were swept away. The people of Jeremiah's day did not heed his warnings and were taken away. **"Behold I have forewarned you."** Matthew 24:25.

The Great Apostasy

Any believer can learn a great deal about the End of Days by studying the book of Revelation, but only those who actually **heed** its words will fully understand it and receive its full blessing. Those who don't cannot expect to survive the Tribulation and be here when Christ returns. The great Apostasy of our generation is the false doctrine of the invisible Return and Pre-Tribulation Rapture. It's a dangerous contradiction to Christ's straightforward teachings on the End Times. It will prove catastrophic for the millions of believers who don't expect to be here when the Antichrist arises.

The pandemic of "Darbyitis"

This "malignant power," as Charles Spurgeon called Darbyism, is like a contagious virus that is infecting most of the evangelical Church today. Our task is to do everything we can to help cure this pandemic of "Darbyitis" with prophetic doctrine that comes directly and solely from the written Word, not filtered through some faulty system of theology like Dispensationalism.

Time to wake up, repent and prepare

Revival is the theme of Christ's letters to the Seven Churches. Nothing is sugar coated. High praise and stern warning are given. Each church has its own set of shortcomings or circumstances to address. Wonderful, distinctive rewards are promised to those who heed His words. It is clear the Lord wants His Bride to be ready for His return but He also wants to build her character and spiritual depth to face the unprecedented challenges of the Tribulation.

Victory in the Tribulation will come from heeding Christ's words

They *(brethren)* **overcame him** *(the Dragon)* **because of the blood of the Lamb and because of the word of their testimony, and they did not love their life, even when faced with death.** Revelation 12:11. **Here is the perseverance of the saints who keep the commands of God and their faith in Jesus.** Revelation 14:12.

The identity of the Seven End Times Churches

The exact identity of each of the Seven Churches may not be readily apparent. Whether they describe churches in the seven regions of the world (the seven continents) or seven types of churches found throughout the world or something else, may not be clear as of yet. At this point I would personally see them as describing the seven churches in the seven major regions of the world.

The Church of Philadelphia is unique in that it is the only one of the seven that is promised to be kept from the test that is coming upon the whole world. **"Because you have a little power, and have kept My word, and** have not denied My name... I also will keep you from the hour of testing hour which is about to come upon the whole world, to test those who dwell on the earth." Revelation 3:8,10. They will be spared the worst of the Tribulation period. This may be because they will have already been tested by trials and have been proven faithful, even though they are not a powerful church. Pre-tribulation advocates insist that only the Philadelphia church is the church of the Last Days, and so is evidence that the Church will not go through the Tribulation, but this contradicts what the text actually says. You could hardly describe the Church in America as having little power. The Lord is telling all of the seven churches that His is coming to them quickly. It is clear that He wants them all to understand (not just the church of Philadelphia) that all seven churches will see Him shortly.

Summary of the Letters to the Seven Churches

One of the strongest points that the Lord makes in these letters is His warning against false doctrine, false teachers, and false practices.

"...put to the test those who call themselves apostles and are not." Revelation 2:2.

"...those who say they are Jews but are not, but are a synagogue of satan." Revelation 2:9.

"But I have this against you, that you tolerate that woman Jezebel." Revelation 2:20.

"So you also have some who in the same way hold the teaching of the Nicolaitans *(authoritarian control by the clergy)***."** Revelation 2:15.

"Wake up and strengthen the things which remain, which were about to die." Revelation 3:2.

"I know your deeds, that you are neither cold nor hot; I wish that you were cold or hot... buy from me gold refined by fire." Revelation 3:15,18.

Some of the main points the Lord Jesus wants the Seven Churches of the Last Days to understand and do:

1. Clean up the false doctrine, false teaching and false prophecy among you
2. Reject the false teachers, false apostles and false prophets among you
3. Do the things you should do and don't do the things you shouldn't do
4. Repent, wake up, hold fast, overcome
5. Those who overcome in the Tribulation will receive wonderful rewards
6. Get ready for the approaching Tribulation
7. Prepare for the soon, quick return of the Lord

Chapter Fourteen

Victory of the Church in the Tribulation

What many seem to forget is that the Tribulation is not just going to be a time of rampant evil and terrible events. Like the fiery furnace of Daniel, it is also going to be a time to see the sovereign power of Jesus Christ on display. We will experience the awesome presence of God as He protects the Church just as He supernaturally protected Daniel's three friends in the fiery furnace, like He protected Daniel in the lion's den, and like He saved Israel from Pharaoh's army at the Red Sea. Unbelievers are going to die by the billions but the Church will be protected and made victorious over the beast even in the most impossible situations. Major miracles may be as common during the Tribulation as they were during the Exodus.

"These *(the ten horns and the beast)* **will wage war against the Lamb, and the Lamb will overcome them, because He is Lord of lords and King of kings, and those who are with Him are the called and chosen and faithful."** Revelation 17:14

"...and those who had been victorious over the beast and his image and the number of his name..." Revelation 15:2.

"Yet not a hair of you head will perish." Luke 21:18.

It's a test that leads to victory and it's victory that leads to the glory of God.

Wouldn't you like to have been there when the Israelites crossed the Red Sea? You wouldn't like to have been there when Israel crossed the raging Jordan River? You wouldn't like to have been there at the battle of Jericho when the walls came tumbling down? You wouldn't like to have been there when Daniel's three friends walked out of the fiery furnace? Wouldn't you like to have been there when Gideon broke the clay lanterns and defeated his enemies against overwhelming odds? Wouldn't like to have been there when Jesus crossed back over the Jordan under threat of death to raise Lazarus from the dead? You wouldn't like to have been there to see Jesus walk out of the tomb three days after being crucified?

Well, here is your chance to see miracles like that. You may be here when the Lord accomplishes a miraculous victory like none that even Israel ever experienced.

The Tribulation will be the Church's finest hour. It will be when the Lord Jesus leads us to our greatest victory over the beast and the dragon. The real point of the Tribulation is that in spite of Satan's greatest efforts, the Church will emerge victorious just as Daniel's three friends emerged victorious from the fiery furnace.

"I kept looking and the horn was waging war with the saints and overpowering them <u>until the Ancient of Days came</u> and judgment was passed in favor of the saints of the Highest One, and the time arrived when the saints took possession of the kingdom." Daniel 21-22.

Nebuchadnezzar's image of gold was a test for everyone. Most bowed down but Daniel's three friends would not. The king tried to destroy them but the Lord Himself showed up and saved them through the fiery furnace. Jesus will show up and save His Church through the test of the Tribulation.

Just like Elijah stood against the prophets of Baal on Mt Carmel, like Daniel walked out of the lions' den, like Job kept his faith through his suffering, like Lot escaped the destruction of Sodom, and Noah was saved through the flood, the Church will pass through the Tribulation victorious because Jesus Christ will be with His people.

"And there will be a time of distress such as has never occurred since there was a nation until that time; and at that time your people, everyone who is found written in the book, will be rescued." Daniel 12:1.

The King of Kings will keep the Church through the Tribulation just as He kept Israel through the Red Sea and the Jordan River and Daniel's friends through the fiery furnace.

"**When you pass through the waters I will be with you** *(Red Sea)***; and through the rivers they will not overflow you** *(Jordan River)***; When you walk through the fire you will not be scorched, nor will the flame burn you** *(fiery furnace)*." Isaiah 43:2.

Chapter Fifteen

Israel's Redemption at Christ's Return

It is not just the Church that will pass through the Tribulation, but the Jewish nation will as well. The restoration of the nation of Israel at the return of Christ is prophesied over and over again in the Hebrew prophets as well as in the prophetic types.

The nation of Israel will be gathered to the Promised Land in the last days.

"For I will take you from the nations, gather you from all the lands and bring you into your own land." Ezekiel 36:24.

The righteous dead of Israel will be resurrected at Christ's return.

"Behold I will open your graves and cause you to come up out of your graves, My people; and I will bring you into the land of Israel." Ezekiel 37:12.

A remnant of Israel will return to God.

"A remnant will return, the remnant of Jacob, to the mighty God." Isaiah 10:21.

The Lord Jesus will reveal Himself to Israel as God.

"Then the glory of the Lord will be revealed, and all flesh will see it together... Say to the cities of Judah,

'Here is you God! Behold the Lord God will come with might…" Isaiah 40: 5, 9-10.

Jesus will build the great temple for the Messianic age in Jerusalem.

"He said to me, 'Son of man, this is the place of My throne and the place of the soles of My feet, where I will dwell among the sons of Israel forever. …describe the temple to the house of Israel…so that they may observe its whole design and all its statues and do them." Ezekiel 43: 7, 10, 11.

At Christ's return the nations will be gathered to Jerusalem and the lost 10 tribes of Israel will be restored.

"At that time they will call Jerusalem, 'The throne of the Lord,' and all the nations will be gathered to it, to Jerusalem, for the name of the Lord; nor will they walk anymore after the stubbornness of their evil heart. In those days the house of Judah will walk with the house of Israel, and they will come together from the land of the north to the land that I gave their fathers as an inheritance." Jeremiah 3:17-18.

The Great Tribulation and Day of the Lord is the time of Jacob's troubles after which Israel's punishment will end and out of which they will be saved at the return of Jesus.

"Alas! For that day is great, there is none like it; and it is the time of Jacob's distress, but he will be saved from it. 'It shall come about on that day,' declares

the Lord of hosts, 'that I will break his yoke from off their neck and will tear off their bonds; and strangers will no longer make them slaves. But they shall serve the Lord their God and David their king, whom I will raise up for them... For I will destroy completely all the nations where I have scattered you, only I will not destroy you completely.**

But I will chasten you justly and will by no means leave you unpunished.'" Jeremiah 30: 8,9,11.

God loves Israel and has promised to rebuild them.

"Thus says the Lord, 'The people who survived the sword found grace in the wilderness—Israel when it went to find its rest.' The Lord appeared to him from afar, saying, 'I have loved you with an everlasting love; therefore I have drawn you with lovingkindness. Again I will build you and you will be rebuilt. O virgin Israel!'" Jeremiah 31: 3-4.

Until the Last Days, Israel will not have a king or temple or a priesthood or indulge in idol worship, but will come to God through Christ in the last days. The accuracy of this prophecy of the history of the Jews for the last two thousand years is amazing.

"For the sons of Israel will remain for many days without king or prince, without sacrifice or sacred pillar and without ephod or household idols. Afterward the sons of Israel will return and seek the Lord their God and David their king; and they will come trembling to the Lord and to His goodness in the last days." Hosea 3: 4-5.

Christ will return to His place until Israel seeks Him. Then He will go forth to revive and raise them up.

" 'I will go away and return to My place until they acknowledge their guilt and seek My face; in their affliction they will earnestly seek Me.' 'Come, let us return to the Lord, for He has torn us but He will heal us; He has wounded us, but He will bandage us.

He will revive us after two days; He will raise us up on the third day, that we may live before Him. So let us know, let us press on to know the Lord. His going forth is as certain as the dawn; and he will come to us like rain, like the spring rain watering the earth.'" Hosea 5:15-6:3.

Judah will have a great victory against the nations in the valley of Jehoshaphat. This may take place before the Lord returns.

"For behold, in those days and at that time, when I restore the fortunes of Judah and Jerusalem, I will gather all the nations and bring them down into the valley of Jehoshaphat. Then I will enter into judgment with them there on behalf of My people Israel, whom I have scattered among the nations; and they have divided up My land." Joel 3: 1-2.

Israel will weep bitterly when the Lord Jesus appears on the clouds as they realize that He is the One whom they pierced.

"I will pour out on the house of David and on the inhabitants of Jerusalem, the Spirit of grace and of supplication, so that they will look on Me whom they

have pierced; and they will mourn for Him, as one mourns for an only son, and they will weep bitterly over Him like the bitter weeping over a first born." Zechariah 12: 10.

But when Jesus comes back on a white horse, there will be a joyous reunion of Israel and their King.

"Shout for joy, O daughter of Zion! Shout in triumph, O Israel! Rejoice and exult with all your heart, O daughter of Jerusalem! The Lord has taken away His judgments against you, He has cleared away your enemies. The King of Israel, the Lord, is in your midst; you will fear disaster no more. In that day it will be said to Jerusalem: Do not be afraid, O Zion; do not let your hands fall limp. The Lord your God is in your midst, a victorious warrior. He will exult over you with joy, He will be quiet in His love, He will shout over you with shouts of joy." Zephaniah 3: 14-17.

The Church holds the key to Israel's redemption

The Church, through Christ, bears its fruit on behalf of Israel. The Jewish nation will reap the rewards of the Church's labor.

"I have sent you *(Israel)* to reap that for which you have not labored; others *(the Church)* have labored and you have entered into their labor." John 4:38.

The 144,000 Jewish Christians of Revelation 7 are the

fruit of the great multitude of Gentile Christians who come out of the Great Tribulation. These 144,000 are the righteous foundation on which the Kingdom of Israel will be reestablished. They are the also the last stone, the keystone of the building that is the Church (Ephesians 2: 20-22), and a covenantal tie between the Church and Israel. We can see this symbiotic relationship as a prophetic picture in the story of Ruth.

It is Ruth who is the key to the redemption of Naomi's land and lineage. Ruth marries Boaz, the kinsman redeemer, and Naomi reaps the benefits of this marriage, just as Israel will reap the benefits of the marriage of Christ and the Church. The fruit of this marriage, Obed, is legally Naomi's own son under levirate law. **"A son has been born to Naomi!"** Ruth 4: 17.

Benjamin and the 144,000

Just as Joseph would not reveal himself to his brothers until his full brother Benjamin was present (Genesis 44:23), so the Lord Jesus will reveal Himself to Israel only after the 144,000 Jewish believers from all twelve tribes are present and sealed (Revelation 7:1-8, 14:1-5). When the 144,000 come to Christ, this will complete the goal of the Great Commission that men from every tribe and tongue and people and nation will be saved, and lastly all the tribes of Israel, including the 10 lost tribes.

"Worthy are you to take the book and break it seals; for You were slain and purchased for God with Your blood men from every tribe and tongue and

people and nation. You have made them to be a kingdom and priests to our God; and they will reign upon the earth." Revelation 5: 9-10.

The 144,000 are not just the offspring of the Church but as Jews from all the tribes of Israel as well, they are also a body representative of all Israel, so they can fulfill a legal contract on behalf of Israel. They can request Jesus to return as their king on behalf of the whole nation:

"**I will go away and return to My place until they acknowledge their guilt and seek My face.**" Hosea 5:15.

Jesus will return only at the request of the Jews:

"**You will not see Me again until you say, 'Blessed is He who comes in the name of the Lord.'**" Matthew 23:39.

The first tribes that sought to bring David back across the Jordan River after the defeat of Absalom, were the 10 tribes of Israel. But it was the tribe of Judah who actually crossed to bring him back as their king even though they were not the first to seek it (II Samuel 19: 8-42). As prophesied in Matthew 23:29, Jesus will return to Jerusalem only at the request of the Jews. First the lost 10 tribes (included in the 144,000), and then when He appears on the clouds, the tribe of Judah (who are the Jews of today) will bring Him back permanently. The Church makes this possible by producing the 144,000 as it fulfills the Great Commission of going into all the world to preach the

Gospel, inadvertently evangelizing the lost 10 tribes of Israel in the process.

The Church will help take the heat off of the Jews during the Tribulation. The beast will be preoccupied with destroying the Church and so will turn from attacking Israel to pursue Christians. **"So the dragon was enraged with the woman, and went off to make war on the rest of her children** *(the Church)...*" Revelation 12:37.

Chapter Sixteen

The Restrainer is the Mystery of Iniquity

The identity of the "one who restrains" mentioned in II Thessalonians 2 has always been very controversial. There is a host of different theories about who this mysterious person or thing will prove to be, from the Holy Spirit, to the Church, the archangel Michael, the Papacy, America, government, the Roman Empire, or a special prophet, etc.

Theories for the Restrainer are usually linked directly to a specific doctrine of the Rapture, whether pre-Tribulation, post-Tribulation, or no Rapture at all. Many teach a specific Restrainer theory as if it were an undisputed fact and all others are clearly in error. The most popular teaching about the Restrainer is that he is the Holy Spirit.

The problem seems to be that the Restrainer is not clearly identified in the text, or is he?

Something is being overlooked

They all seem to make the same mistake in their interpretation of II Thessalonians 2. Finding out what is being overlooked will help us uncover the true identity of the Restrainer.

II Thessalonians 2:1-12

2 *1* Now we request you, brethren, with regard to the coming of our Lord Jesus Christ and our gathering together with Him, *2* that you not be quickly shaken from your composure or be disturbed either by a spirit or a message or a letter as if from us, to the effect that the day of the Lord has come. *3* Let no one in any way deceive you, for it will not come unless the apostasy comes first, and the man of lawlessness is revealed, the son of destruction, *4* who opposes and exalts himself above every so-called god or object of worship, so that he takes his seat in the temple of God, displaying himself as being God. *5* Do you not remember that while I was still with you I was telling you these things? *6* <u>And you know what restrains him now, so that in his time he will be revealed. *7* For the mystery of lawlessness is already at work; only he who now restrains will do so until he is taken out of the way. *8* Then the lawless one will be revealed whom the Lord will slay with the breath of His mouth and bring to an end by the appearance of His coming;</u> *9* that is, the one whose coming is in accord with the activity of Satan, with all power and signs and false wonders, *10* and with the deception of wickedness for those who perish, because they did not receive the love of the truth so as to be saved. *11* For this reason God will send upon them a deluding influence so that they will believe what is false, *12* in order that they may all be judged who did not believe the truth, but took pleasure in wickedness.

The most common mistake of those who attempt to identify the Restrainer

Paul uses some long and complex sentence structures so we have to be careful to make sure we follow and understand exactly what he is saying, and not assume to read something into it that is not really there. The incorrect assumption everyone seems to make about II Thessalonians 2 is that the "man of lawlessness," or the Antichrist, is being restrained from coming. The text simply does not say this. Read it again and note exactly what it is about the Beast that is being restrained.

"And you know what restrains him now, so that in his time he will be <u>revealed</u>. For the mystery of lawlessness is already at work; only he who now restrains will do so until he is taken out of the way. Then the lawless one will be <u>revealed</u>..."

It is not the coming of Antichrist but the <u>revealing</u> of the Antichrist that is being restrained!

This is the most important clue to who or what the Restrainer really is. The text does not say the Restrainer keeps the Antichrist from coming, but restrains him from being <u>revealed</u> in his time. Some may think that this is a slight distinction, but it is actually a huge difference and the key to knowing who the Restrainer really is.

So who is the mysterious Restrainer?

Take another careful look at the text. The true identity of the Restrainer is right before your eyes. It is clearly identified by name right there in chapter 2 verse 7.

"And you know what restrains him now, so that in his time he will be revealed. For the <u>mystery of lawlessness</u> is already at work; only he who now restrains will do so until he is taken out of the way. Then the lawless one will be revealed…"

The Restrainer is the Mystery of Lawlessness or The Mystery of Iniquity (KJV)

The Mystery of Iniquity keeps the Antichrist from being <u>revealed</u>. In other words, the Mystery of Iniquity keeps the true identity of the Beast from being exposed so the world will not realize who he really is. As Paul says, the Mystery of Iniquity is already at work and will be so until he is taken out of the way.

Paul describes the Mystery of Iniquity in II Corinthians 4:4:

"…the god of this world (Satan) has blinded the minds of the unbelieving…"

The Restrainer is actually taught throughout the New Testament (vs 2:5) as the ability of Satan to deceive, but only in II Thessalonians by this name and in this context.

Contrary to what the most popular prophecy teachers say about the Restrainer:

He is not the restrainer of lawlessness
He is not the restrainer of the Second Coming
He is not the restrainer of the Mystery of Iniquity
He is not the restrainer of the coming of the Beast
He is the restrainer of the <u>revealing</u> of the Beast

He is the overpowering delusion on all who have rejected the truth of the Gospel

How and when will the Restrainer be taken out of the way?

At the Last Trumpet when Jesus returns on the clouds for every eye to see Him (I Thessalonians 4:16 & Revelation 11:15). Satan at that time will have lost his ability to deceive the world so that the true identity of the Beast will be exposed for all to see.

So what is the point that Paul wants the Thessalonians to realize and why is it import to us today?

Paul was warning the Thessalonians to not be fooled by false teachers who say that the Second Coming and Rapture can take place before:

1. The apostasy of the Church occurs (2:3)

2. The Antichrist comes to seat himself in the Temple and declare himself god (2:3-4).

3. The restraining Mystery of Iniquity is taken out of the way and the Antichrist is <u>revealed</u>, that is, exposed to all the world for who he really is (2:7-8).

Then and only then will Jesus come on the clouds to gather His saints in the Rapture of the Church (2:1,8) It is important because the same thing is happening today! The Church is being fooled by a false Rapture teaching.

When Christ appears on the clouds, this is not the end, but the beginning of the Day of the Lord

Jesus will gather the Church and then return to heaven where the wedding of the Church will take place (Revelation 19:7-8). In the meantime, Israel will be under attack from the armies of the world led by the Beast. When all Israel comes to faith in Christ, the Lord will then return again to rescue and redeem Israel while pouring out judgment on the Beast and his kingdom (Joel3, Zechariah 12:2-3, 14:2-3).

The removal of the Restrainer is prophesied in Isaiah:

"And on this mountain He will swallow up this covering which is over all people, even the veil which is stretched over all the nations." Isaiah 25:7.

Summary of II Thessalonians 2

- **2:1-3** Christ will not come, the Rapture will not occur and the Day of the Lord will not arrive until <u>first</u>the apostasy (of the Church) takes place and the man of lawlessness is revealed (exposed).
- **2:4-5** The Antichrist will seat himself in the Temple and declare himself God (the Abomination of Desolation) <u>before</u> Christ appears on the clouds at the Rapture.
- **2:6-7** The Mystery of Lawlessness restrains the Antichrist from being revealed and seen for who he truly is "in his day," that is, in the day when he rules the world during the Tribulation.
- The Restrainer in the Greek is described as both an "it" (neuter) and a "he" (masculine). The Mystery of Iniquity is the "it" and Satan is "he."
- **2:7-8** The Restrainer will first be taken out of the way by the appearance of Christ on the clouds, then the Antichrist will be destroyed by the Lord when He comes later to rescue and redeem Israel.
- **2:9-12** The Beast, in accord with Satan, will deceive the world through signs and false wonders. The deluding influence of the Restrainer is allowed by God so as to bring about the full judgment of the wicked.

Chapter Seventeen

The Beast and Mystery Babylon

The reason why the Tribulation will be the Tribulation is because of the dragon and the beast. The reason why Job suffered so terribly was because of Satan. The reason why Israel had to pass through the Red Sea was because of Pharaoh. The reason why Daniel was thrown into the lion's den and his friends into the fiery furnace was because of the Babylonian kings.

The cosmic and world forces of evil will be responsible for bringing in this terrible time of violence and destruction; seven long years of tyranny, war, famine, death, persecution and planetary disasters. Two thousand years of the world's rejection of Jesus Christ and their acquiescence to the lies of godless men will bear its final, inevitable fruit.

Believers have to be ready for the beast

Those who don't expect to be here when the antichrist comes into world power will be taken by surprise. The reason why the Lord gives us so much detail about the Tribulation and Last Days is so the Church will be prepared for it and not fall victim to the powerful satanic deceptions.

"For false Christs and false prophets will arise and show great signs and wonders, so as to mislead, it possible, <u>even the elect</u>. Behold, I have told you in advance." Matthew 24:24-25.

God doesn't want us to be afraid, He wants us to be ready.

The Rise of the beast

The seven year Tribulation will begin with the rise of the antichrist. The first seal of the Seven Seal Scroll of Revelation 6 releases the one on a white horse who goes out to conquer. The first warning the Lord gives us about the Tribulation period in Matthew 24 is to beware of false messiahs. World war follows closely with the opening of the second seal. Then extreme famine, then massive death.

Unfortunately the vast majority of Evangelicals believe they will not be here when the beast makes his appearance, but will be gathered up before. This false teaching will certainly compound the danger to the Church. **"He will destroy the unsuspecting."** Daniel 8:25 (MLB). Those not expecting to encounter the beast are the most likely be his first victims.

"I kept looking, and that horn was waging war with the saints and overpowering them until the Ancient of Days came …." Daniel 7:21-22.

The Fifth Seal describes the deadly persecution of the Church during the Tribulation.

"I saw underneath the alter the souls of those who had been slaughtered for the sake of the Word of God and the witness they bore." Revelation 6:9 (MLB).

We can easily construct a timeline from the Scriptures of the rise and reign of the beast and what believers can expect to encounter and must prepare for.

1. The beast rises to world prominence
2. The Temple in Jerusalem is rebuilt
3. Israel enters into a covenant with the beast in order to reinstate sacrifices in the temple
4. The beast will appear to rise from the dead, giving him a world-wide following
5. Ten kingdoms will hand their power over to the beast as the beast becomes a world dictator
6. The false prophet will show false signs and wonders to lead most of the world astray, declaring the beast as the messiah
7. One quarter of the world's population, one and a half billion people are killed as war, famine, death and persecution follow the antichrist's conquest of the world
8. The beast breaks his covenant with Israel, stops their temple worship and takes over Israel

9. The Abomination of Desolation occurs halfway through the seven year tribulation as the beast seats himself in the temple and declares himself to be god

10. The beast goes on a killing spree and two thirds of the Jews in Israel are murdered

11. The third of Israelis who survive the treachery of the beast will flee to the mountains of southern Jordan

12. The mark of the beast and the worship of his image is instituted worldwide by the false prophet

13. The beast goes on a rampage of persecution against Christians but they continue to witness for Christ

14. The Two Witnesses appear with miraculous powers from God and provide protection for Israel and the Church and a foil against the antichrist for three and a half years

15. 144,000 young Jewish men from the 12 tribes of Israel are converted to Christ and sealed against harm from the beast and the plagues of the Tribulation

16. The beast succeeds in killing the Two Witnesses leading to a worldwide celebration

17. After three days the Two Witnesses rise from the dead and are raptured into heaven while their enemies watch them go up

18. Satan is kicked out of heaven and falls to earth as planetary disasters occur, five months of locust torture, the sun darkens, the moon turns to blood and stars fall from the sky.

19. The armies of the east invade Israel, killing one third of the world along the way, so over half the world's population will die during the Tribulation, a total of over 3.5 billion people

20. The sign of the Son of Man, a spectacular, worldwide rainbow is seen in the sky

21. Jesus suddenly appears on the clouds with the angels, the dead in Christ are raised and the living in Christ are transformed to join them in the air as the world witnesses it all

22. The Mystery of God is finished as everyone on the planet sees with their own eyes that Jesus is the true Lord and Savior and the Church are His true people

23. All Israel comes to faith in Christ when they see Him on the clouds

24. The vast majority of the world are terrified and weep when He appears because there is no repentance for those who have taken the mark

25. The Mystery of Iniquity is vanquished as satan loses his power to deceive mankind and the beast is revealed to all the world for the satanic monster he truly is

26. Mystery Babylon is annihilated as all false religions, philosophies and ideologies are obliterated in a single day at Christ's appearance
27. The Lord returns to heaven with the saints where the wedding of the Church takes place
28. The Seven Bowls of God's Wrath are poured out on the kingdom of the Beast but Israel is miraculously protected from these plagues
29. The Jews ask Jesus to come back as their Savior and King so He appears again on a white horse to rescue Israel and bring judgment on the enemies of God
30. Jesus leads the Jews from Mt Sinai in southern Jordan, over the King's Highway and across the Jordan River into Jerusalem
31. The armies of the world attacking Christ and Israel are completely destroyed
32. The antichrist is killed with a single breath from the Lord and Satan is bound in the bottomless pit for a thousand years
33. The Jews crown Jesus their king, He builds the Messianic Temple and rules the world from Jerusalem for a thousand years

See the list of Last Days Scriptures in the back of the book for Scripture references of these events.

Mystery Babylon

Mystery Babylon has been somewhat of an enigma in

the world of Last Days prophecy with little agreement among prophecy teachers. There are a variety of theories about exactly who or what this actually is. Some identify it with a specific nation or institution like the United States or the Roman Catholic Church.

"Come here, I will show you the judgment of the great harlot...on her forehead a name was written, a mystery, 'Babylon the great, the mother of harlots and of the abominations of the earth.'" Revelation 17:1,5.

A Biblical mystery is that which the world does not understand but is revealed to believers through the Holy Spirit and the Word of God. At the tower of Babel the world turned its back on God to set up their own religions and belief systems in an attempt to build a stairway to heaven. This Babylonian system became the primary tool of satan to manipulate mankind into fulfilling his agenda and destroy the Kingdom of God. Babel means confusion. For some six thousand years confusion has reigned in the minds of men as to who God really is and what is spiritually going on in the Universe. Take a survey on a busy street corner of any American city and ask people who God is. You will get dozens if not hundreds of different answers. That is confusion; that is mystery Babylon. In the first century it was epitomized by the pan paganism of the Roman Empire and in the near future, possibly by a world union of all religions and ideologies lead by the church of Rome, a kind of hyper ecumenicalism. But it is not so much a nation or a city or an institution, but an automatic, universal way of thinking for anyone who does not have the Spirit of Christ. It is the direct descendant of the world wide apostasy at the tower of Babel. It is the blanket blindness that covers most of mankind.

"The god of this world has blinded the minds of the unbelieving so that they may not see the light of the Gospel of the glory of Christ…" II Corinthians 4:4.

The dragon, the false prophet, and the great harlot will cooperate and use this universal blindness to deceive the world into following the antichrist, taking the mark of the beast and bowing down to his image. During the Tribulation it will take the form of an especially overpowering delusion for the vast majority of earth's population.

"The coming of the lawless one is according to Satan's workings, with great power and signs and miracles, all of them false, and with limitless deceit of wickedness for those who, because they did not welcome the love of truth for their salvation, are going to destruction." II Thessalonians 2:9-10.

But in the world of evil there is never real brotherhood. The great harlot will also fall victim to the antichrist as she is betrayed and destroyed in a single hour. The plan of satan is to eventually consolidate his power into blatant devil worship, forcing it on everyone on the planet.

"And the whole world was amazed and followed after the beast; they worshipped the dragon *(the devil)* **because he gave his authority to the beast; and they worshipped the beast..."** Revelation 13:3-4.

Of course we know how this ends. Victory for Christ and the Church and restoration for Israel; the lake of fire for the beast and his followers; and imprisonment in the abyss for the devil and his demons.

Chapter Eighteen

The Three Pentagram Mark of the Beast

As much as anything, victory for the Church during the Tribulation will mean victory over the mark of the beast. Finding out what the mark will actually look like can help believers warn the biblically ignorant in this age when getting tattooed has become a fashionable thing for young people to do.

Six hundred sixty six is the number of the beast and the infamous Mark of the Beast corresponds to this. During the Tribulation, the false prophet will attempt to force everyone to wear the Mark, which is the equivalent of both 666 and the name of the beast. All will be required to put it on their forehead or the hand. Those who refuse it will not be allowed to buy or sell.

The full, undiluted wrath of God will be the judgment of anyone who receives the Mark. Their punishment will be eternal torture and no rest forever and ever.

Those who refuse to worship the beast or his image and refuse to receive the Mark of the Beast will be the first to be resurrected and reign with Christ for a thousand years.

Mark of the Beast in Scripture:

And he causes all, the small and the great, and the rich and the poor, and the free men and the slaves, to be given a mark on their right hand or on their forehead, and he provides that no one will be able to buy or sell, except the one who has <u>the mark</u>, either the name of the beast or the number of his name. Here is wisdom. Let him who has understanding calculate the number of the beast, for the number is that of a man; and his number is <u>six hundred sixty six</u>. Revelation 13: 15-18. *NASV*

Then another angel, a third one, followed them, saying with a loud voice, "If anyone worships the beast and his image, and receives <u>a mark</u> on his forehead or on his hand, he also will drink of the wine of the wrath of God, which is mixed in full strength in the cup of His anger; and he will be tormented with fire and brimstone in the presence of the holy angels and in the presence of the Lamb. And the smoke of their torment goes up forever and ever; they have no rest day and night, those who worship the beast and his image, and whoever receives the mark of his name." Revelation 14:9-12 *NASV*

And the beast was seized, and with him the false prophet who performed the signs in his presence, by which he deceived those who had received <u>the mark of the beast</u> and those who worshipped his image; these two were thrown into the lake of fire which burns with brimstone. **Revelation 19:20.***NASV*

Then I saw thrones, and they sat on them, and judgment was given to them. And I saw the souls of those who had been beheaded because of their testimony of Jesus and because of the word of God, and those who had not worshipped the beast or his image, and had not received <u>the mark</u> on their forehead and on their hand; and they came to life and reigned with Christ for a thousand years. Revelation 20:4 *NASV*

Theories for the mark of the beast

The mark of the beast is one of the most controversial of all the Last Days prophecies. It seems there is a new theory proposed for the Mark almost every week. Let's look at the Scriptures in the book of Revelation that describes the Mark.

Major points of these Scriptures

- It is forced by the false prophet
- It is forced on everyone in the world
- It will be put on either the right hand or the forehead

- Only those with the mark will be able to buy and sell
- Either the mark or the name or the number of the beast must be used
- It is a man's number
- The number of the beast is 666
- There is certain judgment and no repentance for anyone who takes the Mark of the Beast

The Most Popular Theories

- The number 666
- An implanted microchip
- A barcode
- Sunday worship instead of Saturday
- An International ID number
- Rejection of some cult's beliefs
- The name of the beast
- The Star of David
- 666 Blasphemous names
- Any number of specific letters or symbols
- Merely symbolic of something else

Problems with the most popular theories

- **The number 666**: This is valid, since it is given as one of the options, but it is a number, not a mark
- **The implanted microchip**: The mark is said to be put on the hand or forehead, not under the skin. A microchip may be used as well, but that is not a mark

- **The barcode**: This is not really a mark either, but a number in another form
- **A name**: This is valid, since it is given as one of the options, but a name is not a mark
- **A sect or cult's beliefs**: The Scripture is very clear that it is a physical mark on the hand or forehead
- **Merely symbolic**: If it is symbolic, then the text loses its whole meaning and purpose. This is a common tactic of skeptics, cults and sects in an attempt to disqualify Scriptures which clearly contradict their unbiblical beliefs.

What a legitimate theory for the mark should include

- It should be a mark, that is, not a number or a name
- It should be the equivalent of both the number and name
- It should be indelible, like a brand or tattoo
- It should illustrate the number 666
- It should illustrate the name of the beast
- It is a mark that should represent a man

The number must be converted to a mark

- Since we do not know the name of the beast, we are left with the number 666.
- Since the mark is neither number nor name, it must be a symbol that represents the number 666

- I know of no symbol that represent the number 666, but there is a widely used symbol that does represent the number 6

The Graphic Symbol for six

- The pentagram is the graphic symbol for the number six because the pentagram is made up of six parts:

"For the number is that of a man"

- In Biblical numerology, six is the number of man
- Six is the number of incompletion or of falling short of the perfect number seven
- Man was created on the sixth day
- Man's labor was to take place on six days
- Six is the number of human effort
- The major body parts of man are six: head, 2 arms, 2 legs and torso

The Pentagram is a graphic symbol of a man as shown in this ancient occult illustration

The Pentagram is the most widely used occult symbol

- The Pentagram is the graphic symbol most associated with occultist worship
- In paganism, witchcraft, and satan worship, it is often inverted, symbolizing man worshipping satan
- The pentagram can be corrupted, that is, the head turned down toward hell
- It may have a circle around it, which symbolizes the exclusion of God

The Pentagram is universally accepted

- A pentagram by itself simply represents a man. How it is used determines if it has a sinister meaning or not
- The pentagram is the most widely used graphic on the flags of the world
- Pentagrams are commonly used in all kinds of logos, decorations, currencies, and documents
- The pentagram also represents a star, which is symbolic of achievement and high aspirations
- Pentagrams are already used universally, so its use as a symbol of a world-wide organization would be readily accepted, and would not alarm most people

The next step is simple and logical

- Three satanic personalities make their appearance in the Last Days:
1. The dragon
2. The beast
3. The false prophet
- These three make up the satanic trinity that will manifest itself fully during the Tribulation
- The number 666 is a trinity of sixes, one for each member

And now we have the Mark of the Beast

- It is a graphic mark that represents the number 666
- It is made up of a symbol that represents man
- It graphically illustrates the satanic trinity that will take over the world during the Tribulation

And so this is what may prove to be the mark of the beast:

The tri-pentagram mark

The trip-pentagram mark is already in wide use today. Enter "three stars" in any search engine and you will see how some businesses and political groups are already using it. Do a search of "three star tattoo" and you will see that it is becoming an increasingly popular choice for a tattoo. Do not get a tattoo like this is or let anyone you know get one.

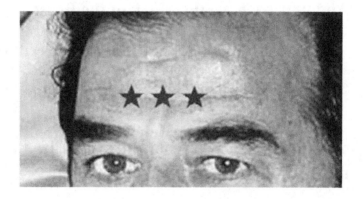

Just as Hitler used the swastika to as an important symbol for Nazism, the tri-pentagram mark may be used as by the antichrist and the ten kingdom confederacy as a symbol to identify their movement and their supporters. Look for the tri-pentagram logo to become increasingly popular in political and military organizations and one world movements in the next 9 years.

The tri-pentagram mark is already showing up on the Euro!

One more point

The great nemesis of Israel was Babylon. According to the prophetic Scriptures, Mystery Babylon, in some form, will rise again in the last days to dominate the world. What symbol does the flag of Babylon have on it today? OK, Babylon doesn't have a flag, or does it?

What country is ancient Babylon in today? Iraq! Take a look at the Iraqi flag:

The mark of the beast could be invisible

There is a growing fad in the tattoo industry of using clear, florescent inks to create tattoos. These are visible only under ultraviolet light. When the Mark of the Beast begins to be used, it may be a florescent ink tattoo, so that the mark will be virtually invisible under most conditions. You could encounter someone with the Mark on their hand or forehead and not even realize it.

Chapter Nineteen

The Lion of Judah and the Day of the Lord

History knows Jesus as the humble, homeless Rabbi from Nazareth who walked the roads of first century Israel teaching and preaching about the Kingdom of God. He was rejected by the world and even His own people. He was crucified, buried, rose from the dead and ascended into heaven. The Apostles witnessed the Lord only as the Lamb of God, the gentle, innocent Son of Man who came to be a sacrifice for the sins of the world so that whosoever believed in Him could be saved. The world has yet see Him as the Lion of Judah. But it certainly will.

The Lion of Judah returns

"Who is this who comes from Edom, with garments of glowing colors from Bozrah, this One who is majestic in His apparel, marching in the greatness of His strength? Why is Your apparel red, And Your garments like the one who treads in the wine press? "I have trodden the wine trough alone, And from the peoples there was no man with Me. I also trod them in My anger And trampled them in My wrath; And their lifeblood is sprinkled on My garments, And I stained all My raiment. For the day of

vengeance was in My heart, and My year of redemption has come.'" Isaiah 63:1-4.

Christ Jesus is both Savior and Judge of all mankind. When He returns, it will be for a different purpose than His first coming. Like king Jehu, His Second Coming will be to execute judgment on the enemies of God.

"He has left His hiding place like the lion." Jeremiah 25:38.

The Beast and his murderous hoards will be confronted by the Lion of Judah as He returns to rescue Israel, destroy the wicked and bring in the Kingdom of God on earth.

"And I saw heaven opened, and behold, a white horse, and He who sat on it is called Faithful and True, and in righteousness He judges and wages war. ...and He treads the wine press of the fierce wrath of God, the Almighty ... And I saw the beast and the kings of the earth and their armies assembled to make war against Him..." Revelation 19:11-19.

The Day of the Lord

One of the key events of the Last Days that confuses many prophecy "experts" is the Day of the Lord. In Biblical eschatology just saying something doesn't make it so, no matter how many respected people repeat it. It must be defined and proven from the Scriptures. If the Day of the Lord is put in the wrong place on the Last Days timeline, it can wreck havoc with the accuracy and understanding of the whole thing. It is a very important clue to the mystery. First, let's look how the Scriptures actually describe the Day of the Lord.

The Sixth Seal describes the sun darkened, the moon turning to blood, terror and wrath.

"I looked when He broke the sixth seal and there was an earthquake, and the sun became black as sackcloth made of hair and the whole moon became like blood; and the stars of the sky fell to earth... 'Fall on us and hide us from the presence of Him who sits on the throne and from the wrath of the Lamb; for <u>the great day of their wrath</u> has come, and <u>who is able to stand</u>?'" Revelation 6:12-17.

The unbelievers obviously see the return of Christ here and so realize in terror that they are about to come under God's wrath.

The Day of the Lord begins after the Sixth Seal's cosmic disasters and terror take place.

"Let all the inhabitants of the land <u>tremble</u>, for <u>the day of the Lord</u> is coming; surely it is near, a day of darkness and gloom, a day of clouds and thick darkness... Before them the earth quakes, the heavens tremble, <u>the sun and moon grow dark and the stars lose their brightness</u>. The Lord utters His voice before His army; surely His camp is very great, for strong is he who carries out His word <u>The day of the Lord</u> is indeed great and very awesome,

and **who can endure it?**" Joel 2:1-2, 10-11.

"The sun will be turned to darkness and the moon into blood before the great and awesome day of the Lord. And it will come about that whoever calls on the name of the Lord will be delivered. " Joel 2:31-32.

Jesus describes the exact same cosmic disasters of the sixth seal at the end of the Tribulation and immediately before His return and the Rapture.

"But immediately after the tribulation of those days the sun will be darkened and the moon will not give its light, and the stars will fall from the sky, and the powers of the heavens will be shaken. And then the sign of the Son of Man will appear in the sky, and then all the tribes of the earth will mourn, and they will see the Son of Man coming on the clouds of the sky with power, and great glory. And He will send forth His angels with a great trumpet and they will gather together His elect from the four winds, from one end of the sky to the other." Matthew 24:29-31.

The Sixth Seal and Seven Trumpets are concurrent

A careful examination of the Seven Trumpets matches the events of the Sixth Seal, showing that the Seven Trumpets are actually an expanded, more detailed description of the Sixth Seal and occurs concurrently.

"The fourth angel sounded, and a third of the sun

and a third of the moon and a third of the stars were struck, so that a third of them would be darkened..." Revelation 8:12.

The Day of the Lord begins immediately after this at Christ's appearance on the clouds. The Seven Golden Bowls of God's Wrath are the Day of the Lord in its full fury. Unlike the Seven Seals and Seven Trumpets, these bowls of wrath are poured out directly from heaven, from the hand of God Himself as a judgment on the wicked and the kingdom of the beast. Malignant sores, rivers turning to blood, scorching sun, painful darkness, demonic spirits gathering the world's armies at Armageddon and:

"Then the seventh angel poured out his bowl upon the air...and the cities of the nations fell. Babylon the great was remembered before God, to give her the cup of the wine of His fierce wrath. And every island fled away, and the mountains were not found. And huge hailstones, about one hundred pounds each, came down from heaven upon men; and men blasphemed God because of the plague of the hail, because its plague was extremely severe." Revelation 16:17-21.

The Day of the Lord includes both parts of the Second Coming of the Lord Jesus: the Cloud Appearance and the White Horse Return. From that day, what the Scriptures refers to the Day of the Lord really doesn't end, ever. It includes the restoration of Israel, the defeat of the antichrist, the Jerusalem Throne judgment, the Messsianic age, the final defeat of satan, the Great

White Throne judgment, the destruction of the old universe, the creation of the new heaven and earth, and even the new Jerusalem and on into eternity future.

In Scripture the term "Day of the Lord" can be used to describe a certain event or day or even hour, or it can be very general, referring to the whole sweep of all the events that results from the coming of Christ. It cannot, however refer to any event prior to His return such as the Tribulation or anything that happens before the Seventh Trumpet. Those who hold to a pre-Tribulation Rapture are certainly confused about where the Scriptures place the Day of the Lord as they erroneously ascribe it to the Tribulation period. A careful study of the Day of the Lord can only place it after the Seventh Trumpet Rapture as Jesus appears on the clouds.

Chapter Twenty

Overview of the Events of the Last Days

The Seven Churches

The Seven Churches of Revelation are not seven ages of the Church as is commonly taught. This idea has no basis in Scripture at all. They are the completed Church as it will be just before the first seal is broken and the Tribulation begins. The purpose of the letters is the revival and preparation of the Church for the test of the Tribulation and the return of the Lord Jesus. Seven is the number of completion and the Seven Churches indicates the completion of the Great Commission.

Acts 1, Romans 11, Revelation 1-3.

The Temple and the Antichrist

Two world events must take place before the Tribulation begins: the rebuilding of the Jerusalem Temple and the military and political rise of the antichrist.

Daniel 7, 9, 11, 23, 24, Ezekiel 28, Isaiah 14, Matthew 24, II John 2, Revelation 6, 13-14.

Birth Pains

The first half of the seven year Tribulation is described as birth pains. They are also called the Four Horsemen of the Apocalypse. Israel will enter into to a seven year covenant with the beast which will allow them to reestablish worship in their temple.

It includes the rise of the antichrist, world war, famine and the death of billions, an unprecedented time of violence and oppression. The great apostasy will occur, when many professing Christians will join the one world religion set up by the false prophet. The world will be divided into ten kingdoms which will then turn absolute power over to the beast. The mark of the beast, required to buy and sell, will probably make its appearance at this time which will consist of three pentagrams.

II Thessalonians 2, Matthew 24, Revelation 5-6.

The Seven Seals

The Tribulation covers all the events described as the Seven Seals and the Seven Trumpets. It will be seven years long and divided up into two parts: The birth pains and the Great Tribulation. The Church will be here during this time. The Seven Seals are:

First Seal: The antichrist appears, is given a crown and goes out to conquer

Second Seal: War

Third Seal: Famine

Fourth Seal: Death (one third of the earth's population is killed)

Fifth Seal: Persecution of the Church

156

Sixth Seal: Cosmic disasters and terror at Christ's return

Seventh Seal: Seven Trumpets as the fall of Satan to Earth and the Return of Christ at the Seventh Trumpet

The Church will actively preach the Gospel and bring sinners to Christ during the Tribulation, even under persecution. They will be victorious over the Beast and the worship of his image, just as Daniel's three friends were victorious through the fiery furnace.

The preaching of the Gospel by the Church will be the cause of Satan's fall from heaven, the overthrow of the kingdom of the world, and lead to Israel's redemption. The Tribulation will end when Christ appears on the clouds at the Seventh Trumpet to rapture the Church and raise the dead in Christ.

Isaiah 2, 12, Hosea 10, Matthew 24, Revelation 5-11.

The Abomination of Desolation

The Abomination of Desolation, when the antichrist seats himself in the Jerusalem Temple, declares himself god and sets up his image for all to worship, will take place three and a half years, or halfway through the General Tribulation. He will break his covenant with Israel and stop the Jewish worship in the temple. Jesus warns those in Judea to flee into the mountains when this happens. Only one third of the Jews in Israel will survive the treachery of the beast.

Isaiah 14, Daniel 8, 9, 11, 12, Zechariah 13, Matthew 24, II Thessalonians 2, Revelation 13.

The Great Tribulation

The Great Tribulation begins with the second half of the seven years when the antichrist seats himself in the Jerusalem temple as god and sets up his image there to be worshiped by all the world. The false prophet will help to empower the reign of the beast by showing false signs and miracles. Persecution will become severe during this three and a half year period; however the Two Witnesses will appear at this time to confront the beast and help protect the Church and Israel. It is also called the "time of Jacob's troubles." The surviving Jews of Israel will escape to the wilderness of southern Jordan where they will be protected from the plagues and persecutions.

Jeremiah 30, Daniel 2, 7-8, 11-12, Zechariah 13-14, Matthew 24, II Thessalonians 2, I John 2, II John 1, Revelation 8-14.

The Seven Trumpets/Sixth Seal

The Seven Trumpets are a subset of the Seventh Seal. They are actually concurrent with the Sixth Seal and give expanded details of the cosmic disasters that will immediately precede the return of Christ. They are a result of Satan's fall from heaven to earth and all the plagues and disasters that will follow. One third of the foliage and sea life will be destroyed, one third of the rivers and springs will be poisoned, and one third of the sun, moon, and stars will be darkened (sixth seal). Satan will fall to earth as a great star and open the abyss, releasing demonic locusts to torture mankind for five months. A 200 million man cavalry will march into the Middle East, killing a third of humanity along the way, making a total of over 3.5 billion people killed during the Tribulation, half of the world's population.

Isaiah 2 and 13, Joel 2, Matthew 24, Revelation 6-11.

The Two Witnesses

The Two Witnesses appear during the second half of the Tribulation. They have supernatural powers to breathe fire and bring droughts and plagues. They will challenge the authority and power of the beast and will play a role in protecting the Church and Israel.

They are killed in Jerusalem, rise from the dead after three days and are taken up into heaven shortly before the Seventh Trumpet sounds.

Zechariah 4, Genesis 19, Joshua 6, Revelation 11.

The Seventh Trumpet

Jesus Christ returns on the clouds at the Seventh Trumpet of the Seventh Seal to resurrect the dead in Christ and rapture the living Church. The Seventh Trumpet ends the Tribulation and the Church age. It begins the Kingdom of God on earth, the Day of the Lord and the Messianic age. The Seven Trumpets are a subset of the Seventh Seal and are concurrent with the Sixth Seal. The Seventh Trumpet is the Last Trumpet of I Corinthians 15 and the trumpet of God of I Thessalonians 4. The last trumpet of the battle of Jericho is a prophetic type of the Seventh Trumpet.

Matthew 24, II Corinthians 15, I Thessalonians 4, Revelation 10-11.

The Return and Rapture

Christ will return as promised at the Seventh Trumpet. Every eye will see Him as He comes on the clouds to rapture the Church and raise the dead in Christ. This is the First Resurrection. He will return visibly in flaming fire with His mighty angels at the shout of the archangel and the trumpet of God. No one will ever again doubt who God is, who His people are and who Jesus Christ is. This will begin the Day of the Lord. The unsaved who have the mark of the beast will be terrified at His appearance because they know that the wrath and judgment of God is about to begin.

Isaiah 40, Ezekiel 43, Daniel 7, Joel 2, Zechariah 12,14, Matthew 24, 26, II John 14, Acts 1, I Corinthians 1, 15, Colossians 3, I Thessalonians 1-5, II Thessalonians 1-2, II Timothy 4, Titus 2, I Peter 1, II Peter 3, I John 2, Revelation 11, 14.

The Day of the Lord

The Day of the Lord begins when Christ returns on the clouds at the Seventh Trumpet. It does not include the seven year Tribulation. It encompasses the Seven Bowls and the White Horse Return, bringing in the judgment of the nations and the destruction of the enemies of God. It is a time of wrath and judgment on unbelievers, victory for the Church and restoration of the nation of Israel. The return of Christ will mean the end of all false religions and ideologies. Darwinism will cease to exist. Mystery Babylon, which represents the world system of false beliefs began at the tower of Babel, will be destroyed in a single day. Every person on the planet will know that Jesus Christ is Lord, but the vast majority of mankind will have the mark of the beast and so cannot repent and be saved.

Isaiah 2 and 13, Jeremiah 25, Joel 1-3, Obadiah 1, Micah 7, Zephaniah 1, Malachi 4, Matthew 13, 24-25, I Thessalonians 5, II Thessalonians 1, II Peter 3, Revelation 11, 14-19

The Seven Golden Bowls of God's Wrath

The Seven Golden Bowls of God's Wrath are poured out on the kingdom of the Beast while the Church is in heaven during the wedding of the Lamb. They are a part of the judgments of the Day of the Lord. Israel will be protected from these plagues as they were protected from the plagues of Egypt. Malignant sores, seas and springs turning to blood, a scorching sun, painful darkness, a massive earthquake and hundred pound hail are poured out on the followers of the beast. Finally, demonic spirits will gather the world's armies into Israel's Valley of Jezreel: Armageddon.

Isaiah 26, Revelation 16.

The White Horse Return

The Return of Christ occurs in two parts: His appearance on the clouds to rapture the Church and a few weeks or months later on a White Horse to restore Israel and judge the nations. After the nation of Israel sees Jesus on the clouds they will repent and turn to

Christ as their Savior and Messiah and then ask Him to return. He will appear at Mt Sinai where Israel will be camped in the wilderness. The Church and the armies of Heaven will return with Him. He will destroy the surrounding armies in the valley of Jehoshaphat and lead the Jews up the King's Highway and across the Jordan River into Jerusalem. He will kill the beast with a single breath and annihilate the rest of the armies of the world in the valley of Armageddon. He will enter Jerusalem through the east gate and be crowned King of Israel by the Jews. When the smoke clears, men will be scarcer than gold.

Isaiah 24, 34-35, 63, Habakkuk 3, Zephaniah 3, Zechariah 8, 9, 14, Malachi 4, Revelation 19, II Peter 3.

The Restoration of Israel

The nation of Israel (the Jews) will be restored as the Kingdom of Israel under Jesus Christ. They will occupy all of the Promised Land from the Euphrates to the Brook of Egypt. Jerusalem and the Temple will be rebuilt. Christ will be their King and High Priest and the feasts and sacrifices of the Temple will resume in a limited way. The age of the Church and the baptism of the Holy Spirit will be over so Israel will once again be under law. The land of Israel will be geologically and ecologically transformed. The lost 10 tribes of Israel will be gathered and restored once again to the tribes of Judah and Benjamin.

Isaiah 60 and 62, Jeremiah 3, 16, 30-31, Ezekiel 20,37-39, Hosea 3, 6, 14, Joel 3, Amos 9, Micah 5, Zechariah 8 , Romans 11.

The Messianic Age

The Messianic Age will begin when the Lion of Judah destroys the enemies of God, judges the nations and restores Israel. The beast will be killed and satan will be locked in the bottomless pit. The Saints will be rewarded and those with the mark of the beast will be cast into hell. Christ will reign from Jerusalem with a rod of iron for a thousand years. There will be no more war, violence or crime. No longer will the earth and mankind be under the Adamic curses. The lion will lay down with the lamb and a child will play with the viper. People will live for hundreds of years as they did before the flood. Every man will eat of his own vine on his own property and no one will take it away. All the nations will come to Jerusalem yearly for the Feast of Booths. The Church will reign with Christ and rule the cities of the world.

Isaiah 2, 4, 12, 24, 56, 60, Jeremiah 3, Ezekiel 20, 34, 40, Daniel 2, 7, Hosea 2, Amos 9, Zechariah 8, 14, Micah 4, Matthew 19.

The Great White Throne Judgment

When the thousand year Messianic Age comes to a close, satan will be released from the bottomless pit for a short while to deceive the nations again and gather them for war against Jerusalem. He will be quickly defeated and thrown in to the lake of fire to be tortured forever and ever. Then Christ will sit on the Great White Throne, the books will be opened and all of the dead in Hades will rise bodily for eternal judgment on their sins and everyone whose name is not in the Book of Life will be cast in to the lake of fire. Those whose names are written in the Lamb's Book of Life will receive eternal rewards according to their good works.

Isaiah 24, 66, Daniel 8, 12, John 3, Acts 17, Romans 8, II Corinthians 2, Ephesians 1-2, Philippians 3, I Thessalonians 4-5, II Thessalonians 1-2, II Timothy 4, Revelation 1-3, 7, 15, 19-20.

The New Jerusalem

After the Great White Throne Judgment, a new heaven and earth will be created. There will be no sun or moon or sea. The New Jerusalem will come down out of heaven to earth where the saints will live with the Lord forever. Isaiah 66, Psalms 105, Matthew 24, II Peter 3, Revelation 21.

Chapter Twenty One

Preparing for Battle with the Beast

From Genesis to Revelation the Word of God goes into amazing detail about all of the events of the Last Days. It is one of the most prolific subjects of the Bible. This leaves no doubt that the Lord wants the Church, especially this generation, to be fully informed and to fully understand what is about to occur in the world. He has been telling us about this for over four thousand years and the time has finally arrived and the generation has finally arrived who will see and experience the consummation of all that has been written. It's a great privilege and a great responsibility to be a believer in Christ in these final decades of the age. However difficult it may be, it will be the Church's finest hour because the Lord Jesus will bring His Bride safely through. By the faithful witness of His people, He will prove to all mankind that He alone is the King of Kings and Lord of Lords. He alone is the truth. He alone is the Savior. He alone is the Messiah of Israel. He alone is sovereign over the affairs of men and He alone has the exclusive right to rule the world.

Heeding, not just reading

It cannot be over emphasized just how strongly the

Lord Jesus warned His disciples about being ready for His return and the events of the Tribulation.

"Behold I have told you in advance." Matthew 24:25.

"Keep on the alert at all times, praying that you may have strength to escape all these things that are about to take place, and to stand before the Son of Man." Luke 21:26.

The letters to the Seven Churches of Revelation are a guide to the last days churches on how to prepare for His return; the revival required to be the kind of Church He wants on the earth when He comes back.

The return of the Lord and the Tribulation are really one event in two inseparable parts. Like giving birth, the Tribulation is the birth pains and the appearance of Christ is the blessed event. It is defined by the Scroll with seven seals. Breaking the first seal begins the test and the seventh trumpet of the last seal ends it with the contents of the Scroll finally unveiled: Jesus coming on the clouds in glory for every eye to see.

The Lord wants us to be ready, not afraid

"Prepare provisions for yourselves, for within three days you are to cross this Jordan..." Joshua 1:11.

Satan is a strategist. He doesn't just do everything compulsively. He is making plans to conquer every power on earth during the Tribulation and we should be getting ready too. We already have the warning and knowledge and commission for it. What we have to do now is take action. We know when it will take place and we know the Lord will give us seven years of plenty. As challenging it will be, it will be far more difficult and dangerous for our us, our families and our churches if we ignore the warning of Christ and do nothing. It is going to happen no matter what we do so it is best to heed His words and prepare. Persevering as a viable body of believers and continuing to preach the Gospel and bringing sinners to salvation during the darkest days of history should be our goal.

"Here is the perseverance of the saints, who keep the commands of God and their faith in Jesus." Revelation 14:12.

The seven letters to the Seven Churches are a field guide to the Tribulation and Second Coming

The book of Revelation was written in a futurity literary style, as if all the events described were just about to happen. This tells us that Revelation was not written directly to any generation as much as the generation that would be here when all these things began to unfold. In other words, it was specifically written to us, to our generation. There is a great deal to be learned from the book of Revelation for any era, but it is the

Tribulation generation that most needs to understand and heed what it says.

The book of Daniel, as primarily prophecies of the Last Days, shares this last generation emphasis and even states this plainly:

"He said, 'Go your way, Daniel, for these words are concealed and sealed up until the end time.'" Daniel 12:9.

Martin Luther admitted that he didn't understand the book of Revelation, which was fine because it wouldn't take place for another five hundred years. But today the words of Daniel and Revelation are being increasingly unsealed, that is, much better understood, because we are now there, we are at the end of the age. The hour glass is pouring out its last few grains of sand.

Even though many believers will be martyred during the Tribulation, the Church as a whole will overcome and be victorious. Because the Gospel will continue to be preached, and the extreme events will convince many of their need for Christ, there will no doubt be more believers at the end of the Tribulation than there were at the beginning. We can expect a great harvest of new believers as we continue to faithfully stand up for Christ and share the good news of His salvation. Knowing what is going to happen and being prepared will also be a great witness to unbelievers.

An example of a check off list for preparing for the Tribulation:

1. Accept the Lord Jesus as your Savior, be born again and have assurance of salvation.
2. Develop a close, abiding relationship with the Lord through daily prayer and Bible reading.
3. Continue to be involved in evangelism, discipleship training, church building, fellowship, missions, Bible study, prayer and Scripture memory.
4. Learn about and heed everything the Scriptures tells us will take place during the Tribulation.
5. Make strategic plans for you, your family and your church to be ready for the entire seven year period.
6. Understand that it is going to be a dangerous and difficult time when we will need to persevere and remain faithful to Christ no matter what, even in the face of death.
7. Keep looking up and believing that our Savior is faithful and true and will return exactly as He promised.

I am not going to go into strategic prepping such as food storage for the Tribulation because that is a subject for an entire book and there are others that have much more knowledge about that than I do. The only thing I would recommend at this point is to acquire some land with a reliable water supply where you can raise food, whether it is at your house or some acreage in the country. We should also have contingency plans to move somewhere safer when danger arises. Some alternate means of communication like short wave radio may be necessary as well. Maintaining contact with other believers in our area and throughout the world will help us encourage and support one another. I would caution, however, about getting involved with some of the end times groups out there. Many of them are violent and dangerous in themselves. Only get involved with groups that are solidly Evangelical with sound doctrine and practices. Avoid groups that are overtly paramilitary, violent, racist, anti-Jewish, anti-Israel, authoritarian, cultish or hold false teachings like the denial of salvation by faith and eternal security. Don't let yourself be manipulated into a situation where you have no control over what happens to you.

The victory of the Church will be through evangelism. That is what will overcome the power of satan and cause his defeat in heaven and his fall to earth.

"I saw Satan fall from heaven like lightning." Luke 10:18.

Our commission is not to go into a bunker and wait it out but to continue to preach Christ to all nations and stand up for His name. Believers who overcome have the promise of wonderful, eternal rewards for their faithful service to the cause of Christ.

"He who overcomes, and he who keeps My deeds until the end; to him I will give authority over the nations." Revelation 2:26.

"Those who have insight will shine brightly like the brightness of the expanse of heaven, and those who lead the many to righteousness, like the stars forever and ever." Daniel 12:3.

"Behold I am coming quickly, and My reward is with Me, to render every man according to what he has done. I am the Alpha and the Omega, the first and the last, the beginning and the end." Revelation 22:12.

List of Last Days Scriptures

THE BEGINNING OF BIRTH PAINS

1. Sudden birth pains: Mat 24:8, Mk 13:7-8, I Thes 5:3

2. The Seven Year Tribulation begins: Jer 30:7, Dan 9:24-27, 12:1,6-11, Mat 24:15-24, Rev 11:3,

3. Gospel Preached to all the World first then the end will come: Mat 24:14, Mar 13:10, Luk 24:47, Rom 11:25, Rev 7:9

4. The Great Apostasy of the Church: Mat 24:10, II Thes 2:3, I Tim 4:1, II Tim 3:1-5

5. Jerusalem will become a cup of reeling and a heavy stone for all nations: Zech 12:2-10

6. The Temple is rebuilt in Jerusalem: Dan 9:27, Mat 24:15, II Thes 2:4, Rev 11:1-2

FOUR HORSEMEN OF THE APOCALYPSE

7. The Four Horsemen of the Apocalypse bring world war: Mat 24:6-8, Luk 21:9-11, Rev 6:1-8

8. FIRST SEAL – Rise of the Antichrist: Dan 7:8, 24,25, 8:9-11, 23-26, 11:12-45, Mat 24:4-5, Mar 13:5-6,21-22, Luk 21:8, II Thes 2:3-12, I John 2:18, II John 1:7, Rev 6:2, 13:1-18

9. World government under the Beast: Dan 2: 34-45, 8:19-26, Rev 13:1-18

10. SECOND SEAL - War: Mat 24:7-9. Mar 13:7-9, Luk 21:9-10, Rev 6: 3-4

11. THIRD SEAL - Famine: Luk 21:11, Rev 6:5-6

12. FOURTH SEAL – Death (1/4 of mankind): Mat 24:21-22, Mar 13:19-20, Rev 6:7-8

THE ABOMINATION OF DESOLATION

13. The Abomination of Desolation by the Beast: Dan 8:13, 9:27, 11:31, 12:11, Mat 24:15, II Thes 2:4

14. Betrayal and takeover of Israel by the Antichrist: Dan 12:41, 9:27, Mat 24:15

15. Decimation of Israel by the Antichrist: Zec 13:8-14:2, Mat 24:15-22

16. The Mark of the Beast (three pentagrams) is required to buy and sell: Rev 13:16-18

17. The False Prophet tries to force all to bow to the statue of the Beast: Rev 13:11-15

THE CHURCH DURING THE TRIBULATION

18. FIFTH SEAL - Martyrdom: Mat 24:9-13, Mk 13:9-13, Luk 21:12-19, Rev 6:9-11

19. Four Winds (Rapture) are held back: Mat 24:31, Mk 14:27, Rev 7:1

20. The 144,000 are sealed as the Jewish part of the Church and the first fruits of the Kingdom of Israel: Eze 9:4,
Zeph 3:12-13, Rev 7:1-8

21. Gentile Church as the Multitude in Heaven coming out of the Tribulation: Rev 7:9-17

SATAN IS KICKED OUT OF HEAVEN AND FALLS TO EARTH

22. SIXTH SEAL – Cosmic Disasters, Terror: Isa 2:19-21, 12:6-13, Hos 10:8, Rev 6:12-17, Mat 24:29, Mk 14:24-25, Luk 21:25-26

23. SEVENTH SEAL – Seven Trumpets: Mat 24:29, Mk 14:24-25, Luk 21:25-26, Rev 8:1-11:19

24. Satan is thrown down from heaven to earth: Isa 14:12, 25:21, Luk 10:18, Rev 8:10, 12:7-17

KINGDOM OF THE WORLD IS REDEEMED AS PEOPLE FROM EVERY NATION ARE SAVED

25. The Mighty Angel appears and roars like a lion: Hosea 11:10, Rev 10:1-11

26. Jesus demonstrates His new ownership of the Kingdom of the World: Zech 14:4, Rev 10:2, 11:15

27. The Little Open Scroll of Prophecies to Israel: Eze 2:8-3:4, Rev 10:2,8-11

28. The Seven Thunders (identity of the Beast exposed): II Thes 2:3-9, Rev 10:3-4

29. The Mystery of God (Christ and the Church) is finished as the Church Age comes to an end: Rom 8:19, 11:25-27, Eph 2:8-9, 5:32, Col 1:26-27, 2:2, 3:4, Rev 10:5-7

30. The Two Witnesses confronting the Beast are killed, resurrected and raptured: Rev 11:8-13

31. Jerusalem earthquake: Zech 14:4-5, Rev 11:13

CHRIST APPEARS ON THE CLOUDS - FIRST RESURRECTION AND RAPTURE OF THE CHURCH

32. Christ is revealed on the Clouds and every eye will see Him: Isa 25:7,40:5, Zech 14:2-5, Mat 24:30, Mk 13:26, Luk 21:27, Acts 1:11, I Cor 15:51-52, II Thes 1:7, Rev 1:7, Rev 11:15-18

33. The First Resurrection: Eze 37:1-14, John 5:25, John 11:23-26, I Cor 15:51-52, I Thes 4:13-18, Rev 20:4-6

34. Rapture of the Church: Mat 24:31, Mk 13:24-27, Luk 21:27-28, John 14:3, I Cor 15:51-52, Col 3:4, I Thes 4:16-17, II Thes 2:1-3, Rev 14:14-16

THE LAST TRUMPET - SEVENTH TRUMPET

35. SEVENTH TRUMPET – Christ comes on the Clouds, the Rapture: Isa 27:13, Mat 24:30-31, Mk 14:26-27, I Cor 15:51-52, Phil 3:20-21, I Thes 4:16-17, II Thes 2:1-3, Rev 11:15-19

36. The Last (Seventh) Trumpet: Joel 2:1, Zeph 1:14-18, Zech 9:14, Mat 24:31, I Cor 15:51, Rev 11:15-18

37. The Kingdom of the World becomes the Kingdom of God: Dan 7:14,27, Rev 11:15-19

THE WEDDING OF THE CHURCH IN HEAVEN

38. The Wedding of the Church: Isa 25:6, Mat 22:1-14, 25:1-10. Rev 19:7-9

ISRAEL DURING THE TRIBULATION

39. The Ark of the Covenant is revealed, reinstating Israel's exclusive covenant: Rev 11:19

40. The Time of Jacob's Troubles – Israel's judgment: Jer 30:4-11, 46:28, Lam 4:22, Eze 20:35-38, Dan 12:1, Mat 24:15-22, Mar 13:14-19, Luk 17:31-32

41. Jerusalem Trampled and Judah flees to the mountains for 3 ½ years: Dan 8:25, 12:11-12, Zech 14:5, Mic 2:12, Joel 3:32, Mat 24:16, Luk 17:22-37, Luk 21:24, Rev 11:2-3

42. The sheepfold of southern Jordan: Eze 20:35, Mic 2:12, 13, Mat 24:16, Mar 13:14, Luk 21:20-21, Rev 12:6

THE DAY OF THE LORD – THE WRATH OF GOD

43. SEVEN BOWLS of God's Wrath are poured on the kingdom of the Beast: Joel 2:30-32, Rev 15:1-16:21,

44. Israel is protected from the Seven Bowls of God's Wrath: Jere 30:7, Dan 12:1, Joel 3:16, Rev 7:3, Rev 12:13-16

45. All Israel accepts Jesus as Messiah: Psa 118:26, Isa 25:9, Eze 37:13, Zeph 3:9, Zech 12:10, Mat 23:39, Luk 13:34-35, Rom 11:26-27

46. The Gathering of the world's armies in the Valley of Armageddon: Eze 38:1-16, Zec 12:3, Rev 16:13-16

47. Babylon/Rome rebels against the Beast but is destroyed in a single day in a fiery conflagration: Isa 20:9, 41:1-15, Rev 17:1-18:24

48. Fall of Babylon's world system of false religions and ideologies: Isa 21:9, 47:1-15, Jer 50:13, Dan 2:34-35, 7:12, Rev 17:1-18:24

DAY OF THE LORD - THE SECOND COMING

49. The Sign of the Son of Man: Mat 24:30, Luk 18:23-24, Rev 15:1,16

50. The Lord returns in glory and wrath: Dan 7:22, 27, Isa 13:6-13, 63:1-6, Joel 2:1-2, 10-11, 30-32, 3:16, 16:15, Hab 3, Zeph 1:14-18, 3:8, Rev 19:11-16,

51. The physical universe is violently shaken: Joel 2:10, 30-32, Hab 3:6-9, Hag 2:21-22, Matt 24:29, Rev 6: 12-17, 16:18-20

52. The Lord returns at Mt Sinai, rescues the Jews there and leads them over the King's Highway into Israel: Duet 33:2, Jud 5:4-5, Isa 10:21-22, 35:1-10, 40:3-5, Hab 3:3-13, Mic 2:12-13, Zech 9:14-16, Rev 19:11-16

DAY OF THE LORD – THE BATTLE FOR THE PROMSIED LAND

53. The Battle of Bozrah. The Lord destroys the surrounding nations: Isa 34-35, 63:1-6, Eze 35, Rev 19:11-19

54. Special Judgment on Edom for their history of treachery against Israel: Psa 137:7, Isa 34:5-6, 63:1-6, Jer 49:1-22, Eze 35, 25:13, Amos 1:1, Oba 1, Mal 1:2

55. Judgment in the Valley of Jehoshaphat (Arabah): Joel 3:9-17, Rev 19:11-19

56. The Lord leads all the Jews back to Israel: Isa 10:21-22, 35:4, 63:1, Mic 2:13

57. The Battle of Jerusalem. The Antichrist is defeated: Isa 11:4, Dan 11:45, Zech 12:1-14, IIThes 2:8, Rev 19:20

58. The Antichrist is destroyed with a single breath: Isa 14:4-21, 27:1, Eze 28:1-19, Dan 7:11,26, 11:45, 9:27, Hab 3:13, II Thes 2:8, Rev 12:20

59. Jesus Christ enters Jerusalem's east gate to receive the throne of David: Isa 4:2-6, Eze 34:23,24, 37:24, 43:1-9, Zec 14:5-9

60. The Battle of Armageddon. The world armies of the Gog/Magog alliance massed in the Jezreel Valley are annihilated: Eze 38-39, Hos 1:11, Zec 14:12-15, 14:12-14, Rev 19:17-19

JUDGMENT ON ALL THE NATIONS OF THE EARTH

61. The heavens and the earth are shaken with violent destruction: Isa 13:10, 24:18-20, Joel 2:10, 3:15, Rev 6:12-17, 16:17-21

62. Defeat, destruction and judgment of all the nations: Isa 2:12-22, 13:6-13, 24:3, 66:15-16, Jer 25:29-38, 30:23-24, Oba 1:15, Mat 13:41,42,49,50, 25:41-45, Rev 20:4

63. Annihilation for the followers of the Beast, men become scarcer than gold: Isa 12:12, 24:6, 34:2-3, 66:15-16, Jer 25:29-38, 46:28, Oba 1:16-18, Zeph 1:18, Mal 4:1

64. Satan is locked in the abyss: Isa 14:15, Eze 28:8, 18, Rev 20:1-3

THE THOUSAND YEAR MESSIANIC AGE

65. Christ will reign in Jerusalem as God: Isa 12:6, 24:23, 60:16,62, Eze 34:30. 43:1-7, Dan 2:44-45, 7:13-14,27, Mic 4:4:7, Zeph 3:19, Zech 8:3

66. Israel and Judah will be united and gathered back to the Land: Isa 11:10-16, 10:21-22, 49:22-23, 66:20, Jer 3:14,18, 31:1-40, Eze 20:33-42, 28:25-26, 34:13, 37:1-38:23, 39:27, 41:27, Hos 1:10-11, Zec 7:7-8, 8:7

67. Gentile survivors will go yearly to Jerusalem for the Feast of Booths: Zech 14:16-20

68. The planet Earth has rest and restoration: Isa 11:6-9, 14:4-8, 51:3

69. Jerusalem and Israel are geologically and ecologically transformed: Isa 2:2, 51:3, Eze 47:1-23, Mic 4:1, Zech 14:4-11

70. The Millennial Temple is built: Eze 40:1-48:35

71. Thousand year Messianic Age of the Kingdom of Israel: Isa 2:1-4,11:1-12:6,14:1-3, 25:6-10, 60, 65:17-24, Jer 3:14-18, 16:14-15, Eze 37:24-28, 34:11-31, Dan 3:44, 7:14, 27, Amos 9:11-15, Zech 14:9, Hos 2:14-23, Amos 2:11-15, Mic 4:1-8, Zeph 3: 12-20, Mat 25:31, Luk 22:30, Rev 20:1-7

FINAL JUDGMENT AFTER THE MILLENIUM

72. After the Millennium Satan is released, defeated, and cast into hell forever: Isa 14:4-21, Eze 28:1-19, Rev 20:7-9

73. The Great White Throne Judgment: Isa 24:21-22, Dan 8:26 12:1, Acts 17:31, Rev 20:11-13

74. The wicked are bodily resurrected, judged, and cast into eternal hell (the second resurrection and second death): Isa 66:25, Dan 12:2, Mat 25:41, Rev 20:13-15

NEW HEAVEN, NEW EARTH, NEW JERUSALEM

75. The Universe passes away with a roar. A new Heaven and Earth are created: Isa 66:22, Psa 105:25-26, Mat 24:35, II Pet 3:10-13, Rev 21:1

76. The eternal New Jerusalem descends out of Heaven to Earth: Isa 60:19-21, 65:17-19, 66:20-24, Rev 21:10-22:5

77. All believers spend eternity with the Lord: Dan 12:2-3, John 14:1-2, I Thes 4:16-17, Rev 21-22

Statement of Faith

1. **The Person of Jesus Christ** - Jesus Christ is fully God and fully man; sinless, born of a virgin, crucified for the sins of the world, raised bodily, alive forever - the one and only Savior and Lord.

2. **Salvation and Righteousness** - Salvation is by faith alone in Christ alone. Spiritual rebirth by personally receiving Christ is essential to be forgiven, saved, and made righteous before God.

3. **The Authority of Scripture** - The Hebrew and New Testament Scriptures are historically accurate and absolutely true; the inspired Word of God and the supreme authority in the Church.

4. **The Nature of God** - The one and only true God is Father, Son, and Holy Spirit; the Creator, Savior, and Judge. God is holy, just, all powerful, all knowing, loving, eternal, and Lord of all.

5. **The Atoning Death of Christ** - Christ died as a substitutionary sacrifice, a complete and final payment for sin so that all who come to Him by faith will be forever pardoned and forever saved.

6. **Sin, Satan, Hell, and Judgment** - Sin, Satan, Hell, and Judgment are objective, universal realities that we can be saved from only through faith in Christ.

7. **The Church** - The Church consists of every believer who has received Christ and has been born again. Every

believer is a priest before God, directly under the authority of Christ.

8. **The Second Coming** - Jesus Christ will return physically to Earth to gather His saints, judge the nations, restore Israel, and establish His Kingdom on Earth for a thousand years.

9. **Assurance of Salvation** - Salvation can never be lost by anyone who has received Christ through faith and has been truly reborn of His Spirit.

10. **The Holy Spirit** - Every person who receives Christ is immediately baptized in the Holy Spirit once and for all time. In Christ we are complete and need no other anointing or baptism.

Timeline of the Last Days According to a 2,000 Year Church Age

On the next day he took out two dinari and gave them to the innkeeper and said, "Take care of him; and whatever more you spend, when I return I will repay you." Luke 10:35

With the Lord one day is like a thousand years, and a thousand years like one day. II Peter 3:8

...and He stayed there two days...After the two days He went forth from there... John 2:40,43

So when He heard that he was sick, He then stayed two days longer in the place where He was. John 10:6

Two "Days" of the Church Age until the Return of Jesus

"I will go away and return to My place" ...He will revive us after two days, He will raise us up on the third day. Hosea 5:15;6:2

2,000 Years

Seven Seals of the Apocalypse

Two part Second Coming
Wedding of the Church
Seventh Trumpet — Appearing of Christ on the clouds and the Rapture
White Horse Return
Day of the Lord

	1st Year	2nd Year	3rd Year	4th Year	5th Year	6th Year	7th Year	Summer	Fall Feasts
	Birth Pains Begin — Four Horsemen			Abomination of Desolation	Great Tribulation		Seven Trumpets	Seven Bowls	

Ascension of Jesus Pentecost

Jerusalem Temple is rebuilt

7 Years of Plenty to Prepare

Thousand Year Messianic Age

Great White Throne Judgment

2,000 Year Church Age Begins — Millennium

30 AD	2016	2023	2027	2030	3030

Church Age of Two Thousand Year "Days" 30 AD to 2030

When the seven years of plenty...came to an end, and the seven years of famine began Genesis 41:53

Daniel's 70th Week
Israel's 70th Jubilee
7x7x70 years since Israel entered the Promised Land

Time of Jacob's Troubles
Judah flees to the mountains
Two Witnesses

End of the Age
First Resurrection
Mystery of God is finished
"But of that day and hour no one knows."
7x7x70÷7

Second Resurrection
New Heaven & Earth
New Jerusalem

Christ returns at the request of the Jewish nation
Israel revived on the Second Day
Armageddon
Judgment of the nations begins

Jesus rules the world
The Jews crown Jesus the King of Israel
Israel is raised up on the Third Day
The Millennial Temple is built

The Week of Human History

Age of the Gentiles		Age of Israel		Age of the Church		Messianic Age
Adam to Abraham		Abraham to Christ		Ascension to Rapture		Millennium
1 Thousand	2 Thousand	3 Thousand	4 Thousand	First Day	Second Day	Third Day

183

The Prophetic Convergence of 2030

World History: 7,000 years, 7 "days" or 70 centuries

Jesus Returns

Garden of Eden — 6000 years or 6 "days" until the 7th "day" Messianic Age begins → **2030 AD**
3971 BC? *

70 is the Biblical number of a full completion of time:
70 years for a normal life span
70 centuries for World history to be completed
70 "weeks" until Israel's redemption is complete
70 Jubilees until Daniel's 70th week begins

70 Jubilees until Daniel's 70th week (7x7x70) → **2030 AD**

Battle of Jericho
1406 BC — 49 X 70 = 3430 years = 2023 AD + 7 year Tribulation =

**"Where is the promise of His coming?" ...with the Lord
one day is like a thousand years and a thousand years
like one day. II Peter 3: 4,8**

Church Age: 2 "days" until Jesus Returns

Ascension of Jesus → **2030 AD**
30 AD — 2,000 years

"Few Bible believing scholars agree when Creation or history began.
Some of the dates proposed near this date: James Ussher: 4004 BC,
Isaac Newton: 4000 BC, Johannes Kepler: 3977 BC, Martin Luther: 3961 BC.

Hosea: Israel will be restored after 2 "days"

Israel's house is left desolate → **2030 AD**
(One year must be subtracted from the sum total of AD and BC since there
30 AD — 2,000 years
is no year zero)

Leviticus 25 Joshua 1-7 Hosea 5:15-6:3 Luke 10:35 John 4:40 John 11:6 II Peter 3:8

© Daniel Speck 11-27-11

Made in United States
North Haven, CT
05 November 2023

43655588R00104